JOSEPH CONRAD
Consciousness and Integrity

STEVE RESSLER

JOSEPH CONRAD

Consciousness and Integrity

NEW YORK UNIVERSITY PRESS

New York and London

Library of Congress Cataloging-in-Publication Data

Ressler, Steve, 1941–
   Joseph Conrad: consciousness and integrity/Steve Ressler.
      p.   cm.
   Bibliography: p.
   Includes index.
   ISBN 0-8147-7405-9
   1. Conrad, Joseph, 1857–1924—Criticism and interpretation.
   2. Consciousness in literature.   3. Integrity in literature.
   I. Title.
   PR6005.04Z7868   1988
823'.912—dc19   87-35109
                                                           CIP

New York University Press books are Smyth-sewn and printed on
permanent and durable acid-free paper.

To Gary Brandwynn

Contents

Acknowledgments

TO Donald J. Marcuse, M.D., an extraordinary secret sharer who healed and inspired.

To Professor John Maynard, who directed the project and the writer without stint.

To Dr. Bernard Jourdan and Dr. Serena Jourdan, who nourished the writer and the work at critical moments.

To Professor Albert J. Guerard, who read the manuscript of a stranger and whose generosity and professionalism were heartening.

THE chapter on "The Secret Sharer" in somewhat different form first appeared in *Conradiana*, Volume XVI, Number 3, 1984. Permission of the editor of *Conradiana* is gratefully acknowledged.

JOSEPH CONRAD
Consciousness and Integrity

CHAPTER ONE

Introduction

THE PROBLEM of integrity, the struggle to affirm self in the face of devastating experience and tragic reality, is at the heart of Conrad's moral preoccupations. Concentrating on five principal works, treated chronologically, beginning with "Heart of Darkness" (1899), followed by *Lord Jim, Nostromo,* "The Secret Sharer," and concluding with *Under Western Eyes* (1910), I seek to demonstrate a coherent and unified thematic development in Conrad's fiction centered on his abiding concern with integrity. By presenting an overview that considers integrity as a developing concept and by placing my analysis of Conrad's moral issues within a perspective of modernism, I hope to avoid the distortions and incompleteness of a fragmentary approach and to provide more precise discriminations than have previous moral critics of Conrad. Although commentators have noted that Conrad's sense of moral and artistic responsibility increasingly disciplined his romantic impulses in outlook and style as his career progressed, and that his intellectual interests widened into larger social and political areas, they have not examined in detail this idea of Conrad's organic development in relation to the question of integrity.[1]

Integrity evolves out of the conflict between Conrad's belief in the self-affirming possibilities of action and the imperative to test the moral substance of his characters. Individualism is the spur to action in the Conradian hero, an urgency to validate selfhood by living up to an ego-ideal. This romantic project motivates, among others, Marlow of "Heart of Darkness" and Jim. In different degrees both men also share qualities and live out experiences that represent many of Conrad's central concerns: solitude, an outcast status, and the irresponsible act that determines the hero's fate thereafter. The test that each man undergoes and fails (the African venture, the *Patna* challenge) precipitates an unresolvable conflict between romantic claims and moral accountability. What becomes clearer over several works is that the quest for identity is simultaneously a search for home—one's birthplace, surrogate parent or family, reconciliation with conscience and the past. Tracing this essential pattern I explore related motifs: impostorship, the protagonist's uncertain sense of self exacerbated when others' perceptions of him jar with the way he regards himself, and profound disillusionment, a crisis that strikes virtually all Conrad's principal figures and that constitutes a turning point in their lives.

Edward Garnett, a reader for Conrad's first publisher Fisher Unwin, who encouraged him and later became a friend, identifies the African experiences as just such a dividing line in Conrad's life, its effects determining his transformation from seaman to writer. He reports Conrad declaring to him that in his early seafaring days, he had "not a thought in his head. . . . I was a perfect animal."[2] In relation to "Heart of Darkness," the words suggest the simplicity, unreflectiveness, and romanticism of Marlow/Conrad before Africa and the shattering disillusionment suffered there, which prepared the way for enlargement of mind. Given its first major statement in the Congo tale, growth of consciousness becomes for Conrad an essential component of integrity, an awakening that is an inescapable tragic burden.

Reflections on the oppressiveness of mind appear frequently in Conrad's writings, both in and out of the literature. Here, in a memorable letter to Marguerite Poradowski, he asserts the onerousness of individuality in thinking people:

> But you are afraid of yourself; of the inseparable being always at your side—master and slave, victim and tormentor—who suffers and causes suffering. That's how it is! Man must drag the ball and chain of his individuality to the very end. It is the [price] one pays for the infernal and divine privilege of thought; consequently, it is only the elect who

are convicts in this life—the glorious company of those who understand and who lament, but who tread the earth amid a multitude of
ghosts with maniacal gestures, with idiotic grimaces. Which do you
prefer—idiot or convict?[3]

Conrad assails self-consciousness because it can result in debilitation
of will. But more distinctive and fearful an aspect of Conrad's mind
is his power of intellectual penetration, expressed as radical skepticism and psychological acuity. Conrad's mastery of psychological
portraiture is of a piece with his profound introspection, what in
Conrad's art Guerard identifies as an archetypal journey within one's
being.[4] When these forces are turned on the self without check as
with Marlow's "wrestling with death" in the Congo or with Decoud
in his isolation on the Great Isabel, the issue can be terrible indeed.
Conrad's penetrating power coupled with an exigency to authenticate values, often by using characters as surrogates to test himself,
accounts for an intellectually daring and emotionally charged quality
in his best fiction that leads to great discoveries and technical
innovations.

I give shape and definition to my argument by placing Conrad,
because of sensibility and style, in what Irving Howe characterizes as
the modernist tradition.[5] Howe's discussion of modernism, although
written in 1967, is still striking in its comprehensiveness and richly
stimulating. "Nihilism," writes Howe, "lies at the center of all that we
mean by modernist literature, both as subject and symptom, a demon
overcome and a demon victorious."[6] Many moral critics, though, fail
to appreciate sufficiently the modernist elements in Conrad's work.
They overemphasize his relationship with nineteenth-century strains,
particularly the English tradition, and they tend to make him more
safe, sane, and "positive," to mitigate the extremes of his doubt and
soften the darker implications of his tragic vision.[7]

Fundamental to this tragic vision, the novelist's biographer Najder
impresses upon us, is Conrad's Polish background. "His own knowledge, and personal as well as national experience, filled him with
skepticism. Again and again he would repeat that he looked at history from a point of view entirely different from that of the British,
who were accustomed to success."[8] Correcting the usual underesti-
mation of Polish experience in Conrad's thought, nevertheless, Najder
is convincing in his assessment that "he was not a nihilist."[9] Despite

enormous hardships, strains, and impaired health, Conrad did strive in his own life for humanistic values. In the fiction, what further complicates and exacerbates Conrad's struggle for belief is the theme of guilt. In its most sustained treatment (*Lord Jim* and *Under Western Eyes*), guilt stemming from a betrayal that is tantamount to murder must receive uncompromising punishment. How to win genuine affirmation despite the awesomeness of this betrayal compels Conrad to the farthest limits of his art. My study recognizes Conrad's skepticism and pessimism as profound though not total. In conflict with Conrad's disbelief is a persistent strain of "hopefulness," an imperative to resist negation and surrender.[10] Though desolation and failure predominate in the best novels and any expressions of redeeming values are muted and qualified, Conrad does reach an earned affirmation in *Under Western Eyes*, for which he struggled half his writing career.

My interpretive method employs close textual analysis that embodies ethical criticism, addressing questions about the meaning, determinants, and consequences of individual conduct, evaluating Conrad's assumptions and judgments as he explores large social, economic, and political contexts. My study rests on the conviction that an inescapable connection exists between fiction and actual life, and the many expressions of this relationship deserve critical attention. Various trends in criticism, of course, dismiss the moral approach as inadequate, falsifying, and exhausted.[11] Deconstructionism, to name a well-known current mode, which regards a literary work as self-reflexive, is limited in my view insofar as it treats the text as a linguistic universe unto itself.[12] To restrict the way literary creations are experienced and understood to internal considerations alone is to impoverish literature. Conrad's language has definite bearings on the external world, and I regard the author as an active presence in his work. My readings seek to illuminate how Conrad's thought, temperament, and life shape his art and are reflected in it, though what is most intimately autobiographical is expressed in subtle, indirect ways, and its explication demands a fine, critical tact.

Conrad's most exacting conception of integrity can be stated thus: in order to attain full integrity as an individual, the protagonist must gain, through extreme experience and prolonged suffering, tragic consciousness and the moral character needed to bear up under the burden of that terrible awareness. Consciousness alone is insufficient because the reality the hero sees now is without protective and sustaining illusions and is crushing in its bleakness. So desolate and withering is Conrad's disbelief and the tragic vision which is its outgrowth that even Conrad at times shies away from its implications. When the hero attains tragic knowledge, can articulate fully its vision and live its consequences unflinchingly *and* can affirm himself in the face of the worst, then the highest integrity is achieved. The cost of this integrity is renunciation of the world: tragic consciousness means the collapse of the belief in self-authenticating action. The patterns and lines of development implicit in the five works that lead to this conclusion are complicated, elusive, and disguised. Only Razumov of *Under Western Eyes* achieves this ultimate integrity, and all the other Conradian heroes, measured against him, are either limited or fall short in some important way. No former study has treated in sustained fashion growth of consciousness as an essential value by which to judge all Conrad's major heroes. And, I might add, this same sequence of disillusionment followed by enhanced consciousness applies to Conrad's two most impressive heroines, Emilia and Natalie. In a minor key, Natalie grows into a mature integrity that complements Razumov's stature. Reality inflicts severe wounds on her, but unlike Emilia she is capable of affirmation primarily because she can return home to do her patriotic work, whereas Emilia remains in privileged exile, cut off from the deeper life rhythms of the country. Thus, the rounding off of Natalie's drama is a more artistically successful rendering of Conrad's vision than is his portrayal of Mrs. Gould's fate.

I accept the generally held view that Conrad's art declined after *Under Western Eyes*. The advocates of this position describe, without adequately accounting for, the changes that appear in his work which mark it as different and inferior.[13] I have submitted an argument— indeed my study has been shaped in part toward this end—that seeks to elucidate the underlying forces, the internal tensions in the literature itself, that make Conrad's falling off a logical outgrowth of his artistic and intellectual concerns. Such is the resolution in *Under Western Eyes*, its esthetic finality, that no further original and compelling fiction could follow.

Betrayal, guilt, and punishment are intrinsic to Conrad's theme of integrity. I treat them as part of an interrelated and evolving whole over the span of five major works. Where I differ from other explicators is in considering the subject of betrayal not as repetition or variation but as one continuing theme, following a logical and progressive development, each fiction being a more advanced working out of the principal conflicts. Briefly stated, the crucial problem for Conrad was to clarify and then to dramatize explicitly the betrayal most charged emotionally for him, that betrayal which the hero recognizes or is compelled to recognize as a violation of conscience. This awareness destroys the hero's sources of individualism. To transgress against society and its laws is irreparably damaging but not fatal so long as the hero can maintain his inner self-justification, invariably rooted in an ideal self-conception. The ultimate wrong is the betrayal of the double in his direct appeal for trust. Brought to full imaginative realization only in *Under Western Eyes*, this situation involves the hero giving up the other man to death at the same time that the act strikes against a vital part of himself. The necessity of remorse and punishment is undeniable, but to admit feelings of remorse to consciousness, Conrad fears, will bring collapse. This self-repudiation means a loss of identity based on will and action. What follows is the abyss of nihilism, and to resist its terrible effects (despair, disintegration, suicide) Conrad must discover resources of affirmation in which he can believe.

I examine in particular two major currents that give definition to Conrad's art, his romantic and tragic impulses. By a "romantic" work of fiction in Conrad I mean essentially one which struggles to retain belief in the self-affirming possibilities of action and serves to release energies attendant on that belief, given Conrad's stronger inclination toward pessimism and skepticism. By "tragic" I mean a creation in which Conrad's darker, nihilistic strain predominates, a modernist redefinition of traditional tragedy. Of course, these dual impulses coexist in artistic tension in each text under study, but I attempt to show the complementary relationship between two pairs of fictions, the tragic "Heart of Darkness" and the romantic *Lord Jim,* the romantic "The Secret Sharer" and the tragic *Under Western Eyes.* The works in each pairing are complementary and interdependent not merely because of their linked and overlapping periods of composition, but because the romantic fiction affords Conrad's imagination release, expansiveness, and consolation in relation to the oppressiveness and exactions of the tragic work.

CHAPTER TWO

"Heart of Darkness": Loss of Self

I

MARLOW cannot explain his impulse to go to Africa, an indication that some unknown but deeply significant motivation is at work. This urge is pressing enough to have him enlist the aid of relatives. Marlow himself is uneasy by his compromising of principle and pride, and immediately suspicion is cast on his moral character, his motives, and the whole idea of a dangerous venture into the wilderness. On the face of it, the undertaking seems impractical, unprofitable, and reckless, an ordeal apparently without purpose except as a fulfillment of a boyhood wish for romantic daring. Marlow expresses anxiety if not guilt about the means he employs to land the Congo job and can find no justification for his actions. Tension is already established between Marlow's conscious awareness and secret desires. His urgency to reach the Congo suggests a compulsion to force one's experience to an extreme, a necessity of character to seek opposition and challenge in order to authenticate selfhood.

During tea conversation with his aunt, Marlow learns that she had presented a flattering but false description of him to the Company.[1] She had advanced him as "an exceptional and gifted creature," "one of the Workers," "something like an emissary of light, something like

a lower sort of apostle."[2] This portrait of himself as a superior being
inspires a vague discomfort in Marlow. "In the street—I don't know
why—a queer feeling came to me that I was an impostor" (59–60).
Apprehensive that he is not what he is made out to be, nevertheless,
Marlow is acquiescent as his aunt creates a personality for him. This
incident is the first of several which constitute a significant pattern,
a motif of imposture. Although Marlow finds the way others see him
objectionable, he says nothing to counter their impressions. And this
passivity hints at a deficiency of character more serious than self-
ignorance.

Pretense continues for Marlow as he steps into the identity of a
Company man, achieving his appointment because of the sudden death
of a Captain Fresleven: "Nobody seemed to trouble much about
Fresleven's remains, till I got out and stepped into his shoes" (54).
The element of masquerade is evident by the way individuals view
Marlow in Africa. When he arrives at the first Company station,
Marlow is taken for the usual white man by the black sentry guarding
a chain gang of exhausted slaves. The guard, "with a large, white,
rascally grin, and a glance at his charge, seemed to take me into partnership in his exalted trust. After all, I also was a part of the great
cause of these high and just proceedings" (65). At the Central Station, Marlow allows the white brickmaker who makes no bricks to
believe what he will as to his, Marlow's, power and higher connections in the Company. Marlow confesses that he went near enough
to a lie by "letting the young fool there believe anything he liked to
imagine as to my influence in Europe. I became in an instant as much
of a pretense as the rest of the bewitched pilgrims" (82). Despite
Marlow's declaration that he abhors lies, he does nothing to correct
what he feels to be inaccurate and repugnant impressions of him.
Failure to challenge these public definitions suggests a lack of assured identity. At the same time, this image of Marlow as a white
official in an exploitative business forces the reader to see him as an
accomplice to the operation. Although Marlow feels detached from
the Company's sordid activities and morally superior to the blatantly
corrupt whites, he is, in fact, a participant, despite his lack of profit
motive. To acknowledge, as others do, that he is one of them, that
he is guilty of complicity, would debase him in his own eyes. In this
respect, he is similar to Jim in the *Patna* lifeboat trying to dissociate

himself from the "three dirty owls" who deserted. Marlow does not act to sever himself from these contaminating contacts, to act in opposition and to define himself in his own terms, until after Kurtz's death. Loyalty to Kurtz, in effect, helps forge Marlow's moral identity.

Presenting points of similarity between Marlow and Kurtz, establishing them as doubles, is Conrad's way of leading up to the heart of their relationship, the meaning and consequences of Marlow's identification with Kurtz. Both men have a sentimental and devoted woman in their lives, Marlow's aunt and Kurtz's Intended. Each woman is blindfolded by illusion to the actual nature of colonial enterprise, and each has a romantic conception of the man she sees off into the wilderness. Both men received their appointments through family patronage. The agent at the Central Station praises Kurtz in language that echoes the description of Marlow his aunt presented to the Company. The official says that Kurtz "is a prodigy. . . . He is an emissary of pity, and science, and progress, and devil knows what else. We want for the guidance of the cause intrusted to us by Europe, so to speak, higher intelligence, wide sympathies, a singleness of purpose." And the agent explicitly joins the two men by claiming to Marlow, "You are of the new gang—the gang of virtue. The same people who sent him specially also recommended you" (79). However exaggerated this characterization, it serves to call into question their moral idealism. Kurtz believes his rhetoric of progress and Christian civilization, and Marlow professes too insistently his belief in the redeeming idea of efficiency and work. Both men, in addition, are seduced by the power of language. When Marlow reads Kurtz's seventeen-page pamphlet, he is intoxicated by the inflated prose, "burning noble words." The peroration "gave me the notion of an exotic Immensity ruled by an august Benevolence" (118). Here, Marlow is rhapsodizing, Conrad satirizing Marlow implicitly; the sentence with its capitalized abstractions suggests also Conrad mocking his own stylistic excesses. As a man without restraint, Kurtz is also an extremist in language. His eloquence convinces most—including himself—that his altruistic motives are genuine. However, Kurtz is no hypocrite. "He could get himself to believe anything—anything," says his cousin. The devastating postscriptum to Kurtz's pamphlet exposes the baseness masked by the vocabulary of high aspiration. But Conrad undercuts even the possibility that moral considerations prompted Kurtz's mission in the first place. When Marlow returns to Brussels, he learns through the Intended that Kurtz did not come from a wealthy background. "He had given me some reason to infer that it was his impatience of comparative poverty that drove him out there" (159). The passion for success, power, and fame underlay Kurtz's crusade to the Congo, a passion he conceals from himself. Like Marlow, Kurtz is an impostor, unaware of his deepest nature, and both are suspect in their moral idealism.

Before he actually meets Kurtz, Marlow is drawn to him by the various agents' descriptions and comments. His growing interest has a profoundly personal basis, and he fastens on those aspects of work and idealized action in the man which relate most intimately to himself. Marlow lauds work as a means of attaining self-knowledge through the solitary test it affords one's capacities: "I don't like work—no man does—but I like what is in the work—the chance to find yourself. Your own reality—for yourself, not for others—what no other man can ever know" (85). Apparently, Kurtz at one time also spoke of work as a means of measuring self. Marlow overhears an agent say to his uncle about Kurtz: "He has asked the Administration to be sent there with the idea of showing what he could do" (89). A man of principles himself, Marlow sees in Kurtz someone whose convictions were subjected to the most demanding test of experience. Marlow is "curious to see whether this man, who had come out equipped with moral ideas of some sort, would climb to the top after all and how he would set about his work when there" (88). If Kurtz can fulfill Marlow's expectations, emerge as an honorable and exemplary worker, a man of stature transcending the pervading corruption, perhaps in Marlow's eyes his own Congo experience will be redeemed, will be provided a meaning and purpose, his own values and secret hopes reaffirmed. Marlow's curiosity is rooted in his own most deeply felt concerns. Identification with Kurtz is already marked, and Marlow's journey into the interior, toward Kurtz, begins to shape itself as a quest for self-confrontation.

Before Marlow can encounter his other self, he must be receptive and vulnerable; he must first shed his impostor's role. The man who stepped into Fresleven's shoes must now discard them. The black helmsman, educated by Marlow's predecessor and so identified with the Dane, is mortally speared during the attack on the steamboat. This manner of death recalls the spear thrust that ended Fresleven's life and gave Marlow an unearned captaincy, an appointment tainted further by the mercenary activities of the Company. The blood on Marlow's shoes is also Fresleven's blood, and Marlow's flinging these shoes overboard suggests a casting off of a dead self, dead because false and imposed. A vital part of Marlow has been quickened to life. Once Marlow actually meets Kurtz and draws into intimate alliance with him, he starts to become morally dissociated from the rest of the Company people. What had been foreshadowed symbolically by throwing away the bloody shoes now begins to be acted out. At the Inner Station white officials are already scheming against the dying Kurtz. Marlow is repulsed by the manager's hypocrisy in accepting Kurtz's ivory but deploring his incautious and "unsound method." Marlow refuses to assent to the manager's abject dismissal of Kurtz and declares with emphasis that "Kurtz is a remarkable man." Immediately, the manager disowns Marlow for this even slight advocacy. "My hour of favour was over; I found myself lumped along with Kurtz as a partisan of methods for which the time was not ripe: I was unsound! Ah! but it was something to have at least a choice of nightmares" (138). The Russian youth, Kurtz's follower, shyly beseeches Marlow as a "brother seaman" to preserve the master's reputation. A man's public name and an appeal for trust are always precious for Conrad. Thus implored, Marlow articulates a dim feeling that will deepen into the most profound loyalty: "As it happens, I am Mr. Kurtz's friend—in a way" (138).

II

THE NEED to test and discover self is inextricably linked with the story's crisis of values. Conrad's conscious struggle for affirmation is constantly undermined by his ironic skepticism and sense of unbelief. These opposing strains find pointed expression in Conrad's treatment of Marlow, where the author identifies with his narrator and often speaks directly through him, while at the same time implicitly criticizing his hero's most insistently voiced beliefs and callow responses to experience. In tension with his romantic impulses, the

conventional side of Marlow's character is conditioned by and reflective of his profession. On many points Conrad supports his captain's advocacy of work. However, Marlow strains to idealize work,
to raise a private creed to a transcendental value. But Marlow's Congo
experience and Conrad's vision prove the activity of work to be only
a temporary and unreliable safeguard and the values of work to be
moral formulas unsustainable before the most terrible truths.

Once in the jungle, Marlow is shocked and dismayed at the mockery of work and the brutal realities of European oppression. At the
Central Station, he turns to his wrecked steamboat for comfort and
security. "I went to work the next day, turning, so to speak, my back
on that station. In that way only it seemed to me I could keep my
hold on the redeeming facts of life. Still, one must look about sometimes; and then I saw this station, these men strolling aimlessly about
in the sunshine of the yard. I asked myself sometimes what it all
meant" (75–76). Marlow is not prepared to admit that there is no
moral purpose behind what he sees. Gradually, he is affected by the
absurdity of the station, the jungle, and by his increasing alienation.
But when he and his foreman seize upon the imminent arrival of
their long-delayed rivets, they dance like gay lunatics, rescued from
their enforced idleness and gnawing demoralization. Those rivets hold
more than Marlow's steamboat together. The wilderness, recounts
Marlow,

> looked at you with a vengeful aspect. I got used to it afterwards; I did
> not see it any more; I had no time. I had to keep guessing at the
> channel. . . . When you have to attend to things of that sort, to the
> mere incidents of the surface, the reality—the reality, I tell you—fades.
> The inner truth is hidden—luckily, luckily. (93)

When Marlow feels his kinship with the savages on shore, preoccupation with work enables him to suppress his urge to join "this wild
and passionate uproar." To resist the awful truth and attraction of
unconscious feelings, Marlow insists a man "must meet that truth
with his own true stuff—with his own inborn strength. Principles
won't do. . . . No; you want a deliberate belief" (97). The values of
work, however, do not prove to be that deliberate belief, for Marlow
must confront Kurtz alone in the night jungle, without the refuge
of his boat.

Marlow never explicitly repudiates his idealistic faith, and the reader is forced to trust the tale (Conrad's artistic rendering of "Heart of Darkness") rather than the teller. The meditative Marlow sitting Buddha-like on the deck of the *Nellie* about to recite his story seems to retain many of the same moral attitudes as those of the uninitiated Marlow of his own narrative. Certainly, he has undergone a profound experience, but he does not appear to have understood it fully or its effect on him. "It was the farthest point of navigation and the culminating point of my experience. It seemed somehow to throw a kind of light on everything about me—and into my thoughts. It was somber enough, too—and pitful—not extraordinary in any way—not very clear either" (51). By presenting Marlow as a hesitant and uncertain interpreter, Conrad invites the reader to pursue his, the reader's, own meaning and, indirectly, to be skeptical of Marlow's commentary. Marlow gives voice to what Conrad's art implies: certitude in perception and ethical formulation, the tacit assumption that certitude is possible in assessing experience, has become untenable.

Marlow's exposure to the Congo brings into immediate and painful focus his previous knowledge about the ugly facts inherent in colonization. Nevertheless, he still maintains a steadfast belief that the modern version of progress and subjugation is redeemed by an informing moral purpose. As preface to his personal narrative, Marlow dismisses the Romans as mere conquerors, possessing only brute force and lacking in any administrative capacity. But Marlow's devaluation of the Romans in favor of the modern colonizer is unconvincing. Nothing in "Heart of Darkness," beyond Marlow's assertion and his praise of the English red on the map in the Company's Brussels office, persuades one that the contemporary civilizer is any less brutal or more efficient than the Roman predecessor Marlow depicts. No portrait of an admirable Western colonizer is presented. According to Marlow, however, the current empire-builder is slightly different. "What saves us is efficiency. . . . What redeems it [colonization] is the idea only. An idea at the back of it; not a sentimental pretense but an idea; and an unselfish belief in the idea—something you can set up, and bow down before, and offer a sacrifice to" (50–51). Nothing suggests that Marlow is being ironic when he praises devotion to a cause, but Conrad's image of worship is ironic, turning back on the speaker. It suggests the corrupting influence of the idea, the idea raised to a false idol and possessing the man—fanaticism—and it specifically anticipates the extremist Kurtz being worshiped in the jungle. Like his double, Marlow is also blinded by his own high-sounding rhetoric.

Of necessity, Marlow is oriented to surface appearance and straightforward facts. Consequently, he is warmly responsive to those details which seem to confirm his mariner's view of things, and it is this impercipience in Marlow which Conrad treats ironically. Disheartened by the chaos at the Central Station and the suffering of the blacks, Marlow is revivified by his meeting with the Company's chief accountant, dressed in crazy but neatly elegant attire. Immediately, Marlow admires the man. "Yes; I respected his collars, his vast cuffs, his brushed hair. His appearance was certainly that of a hairdresser's dummy; but in the great demoralization of the land he kept up his appearance. That's backbone. His starched collars and got-up shirt-fronts were achievements of character. . . . And he was devoted to his books, which were in apple-pie order" (68). Despite a show of respectability and discipline, this model worker is hollow, unfeeling, and morally callous, annoyed at the sick agent dying in his hut whose groans disturb his attention to bookkeeping. Since Marlow believes in the idea the man seems to represent, he must believe in the man. This "hairdresser's dummy" is a striking anticipation of Kurtz. An incoming caravan creates a tumult and the accountant reveals displeasure: "When one has got to make correct entries, one comes to hate those savages—hate them to the death" (70), a foreshadowing of Kurtz's "Exterminate all the brutes!"

Again, Conrad underscores ironically Marlow's response when the skipper exults at finding a sixty-year-old book, *An Inquiry into some Points of Seamanship:* "You could see there a singleness of intention, an honest concern for the right way of going to work, which made these humble pages, thought out so many years ago, luminous with another than a professional light. The simple old sailor, with his talk of chains and purchases, made me forget the jungle and the pilgrims in a delicious sensation of having come upon something unmistakably real" (99). There is a certain pathos in Marlow's relief and reassurance at embracing a familiar object, a frail, outdated, technical manual that rekindles belief in a recognizable, ordered world. Marlow believes it an "extravagant mystery" that the marginalia appear to be in cipher. Of course, he is blind to the moral insignificance of this particular kind of inquiry, a book whose applicability to his extreme situation is as absurd as its appearance in the jungle. And the Englishman's enthusiasm is a reminder that he fails constantly to grasp the real mystery. Indeed, this younger Marlow is like a simple old sailor himself when it comes to exploring moral complexity. He could have written the book he found but not "Heart of Darkness."[3] He is unable to penetrate to the heart of his experience because to do so would involve a crisis of belief, a loss of values so utterly an outgrowth and expression of his nature as to shatter him.

III

WHAT Marlow means by one's inborn strength, the "deliberate belief" that he asserts is needed to resist succumbing to primitive inner forces, is never articulated clearly or convincingly. Behind Marlow's desperate insistence is an urgency to discover within himself those resources and moral values that constitute conscience. Both Conrad and Marlow are inordinately fearful of a loss of self-control. What Conrad writes in the preface to *A Personal Record* could serve just as well for Marlow:

> It may be my sea training acting upon a natural disposition to keep good hold on the one thing really mine, but the fact is that I have a positive *horror* of losing even for one moving moment that full possession of myself which is the first condition of good service.[4] (emphasis added)

Conrad's fear extends also to his activity as an artist. In language that recalls moral concerns in "Heart of Darkness," Conrad speaks of the risks inherent in the creative process itself: "In that interior world where his [the artist's] thought and his emotions go seeking for the experience of imagined adventures, there are no policemen, no law, no pressure of circumstance or dread of opinion to keep him within bounds. Who then is going to say Nay to his temptations if not his conscience?"[5] Of course, to pose this question rhetorically is not to answer it with assurance. In "Heart of Darkness" 's organizing principle of the journey, what Guerard calls also the "journey within," a descent into the unconscious, Conrad is able to dramatize what he dreaded, the loss of self-control with its many implications.

Throughout the story there is an anxious questioning into the nature of restraint. In the Congo, without societal checks (law, public opinion, friends), the temptation to act out forbidden desires or to transgress permitted bounds is all the more real. Work is certainly a restraining force, and up to a point necessary activity bridles excess and encourages self-discipline. Seeing that his ship is safe also constitutes Marlow's safety. During the attack on the steamboat, the black helmsman is killed when he leaves the wheel to fire out the window. Marlow laments: "Poor fool! If he had only left that shutter alone. He had no restraint, no restraint—just like Kurtz" (119). He dies in one sense because of dereliction of duty. (In this respect he bears comparison with the faithful *Patna* helmsmen in *Lord Jim*, admirable examples of steadfastness in crisis.) However contained Marlow is by work, he also senses the increasing pressures from without and within that undermine self-control. He is amazed that the cannibals on board did not overpower the pilgrims to assuage their hunger.

> And I saw that something restraining, one of those human secrets that baffle probability, had come into play there. . . . Restraint! What possible restraint? Was it superstition, disgust, patience, fear—or some kind of primitive honour? No fear can stand up to hunger, no patience can wear it out, disgust simply does not exist where hunger is; and as to superstition, beliefs, and what you may call principles, they are less than chaff in a breeze. . . . It takes a man all his inborn strength to fight hunger properly. (104–5)

Hunger is associated with the story's important and recurring metaphor of hollowness, suggestive of a psychic state, a feeling of absence of self. When Marlow looks into his own soul, he will have to resist a terrible hunger, a stark vacancy that threatens to annihilate him.

The two aspects of the unconscious explored in "Heart of Darkness," its passion and its emptiness, are represented with different emphases in Kurtz and Marlow. For the Englishman, however, the temptation to atavism is superficial and unconvincing. Reversion to savagery is not the urgent danger for him. He is too bound to rationality and control, too circumscribed by the conventional; his nature is too rigid and inflexible, and he lacks Kurtz's intensity of passion. If savage instincts threatened to overwhelm Marlow, it would probably result not in submission, which would be intolerable, but in breakdown and madness, a splitting apart of the personality. Kurtz, of course, succumbs to primitive impulses. The skulls Marlow sees on stakes in front of Kurtz's hut

> only showed that Mr. Kurtz lacked restraint in the gratification of his various lusts, that there was something wanting in him—some small matter which, when the pressing need arose, could not be found under his magnificent eloquence. Whether he knew of this deficiency himself I can't say. I think the knowledge came to him at last—only at the very last. But the wilderness . . . had whispered to him things about himself which he did not know, things of which he had no conception till he took counsel with this great solitude—and the whisper had proved irresistibly fascinating. It echoed loudly within him because he was hollow at the core. (131)

If uncontrolled, lust for power and self-gratification, whose source is unconscious, leads ultimately to the demonic. The hollowness of Kurtz and other corrupt agents suggests an absence of conscience, what amounts to a lack of character. But another expression of hollowness is implicit in Conrad's portrayal of Marlow. Guerard signifies this menace of the primitive self, apathy and inertia, as the more fearful darkness of soul for Conrad because it is associated with death. "There is a darkness of passivity, paralysis, immobilization; it is from the state of entranced languor rather than from the monstrous desires that the double Kurtz, this shadow, must be saved."[6] It is not from "entranced languor" that Kurtz must be saved; he is crawling back to the hellish night ceremonies when Marlow intercepts him. Rather the "hollowness at the core" in Marlow refers to an inner void that can bring on psychic dissolution.

Kurtz is Marlow's double by virtue of a certain temperamental affinity, apparently shared values, and the Congo experience. The inevitable identification with Kurtz becomes more pronounced once Marlow actually confronts him. More than an alter ego, Kurtz is also a projection and symbol of Marlow's unconscious, that feared part of himself he represses. The nightmarish struggle between the two men in the jungle marks the dramatic and psychological climax. Here at the Inner Station the surface journey culminates in an interior one. Historical retrogression merges into the psychological; the journey backward to a primordial state, the dissolution of form, has its counterpart in psychological regression, the gradual loss of adult consciousness and a descent into the primitive and chaotic self. When Marlow chases after the crawling Kurtz, reversion is suggested by Kurtz's animal posture and by Marlow's irrational chuckling, by his circumventing Kurtz "as though it had been a boyish game" (142). This theme of regression implies that Marlow, quite unaware, is driven to pursue not merely Kurtz but his own unconscious self. When he looks into Kurtz's mad, struggling soul, he stares also into his own. "But his soul was mad. Being alone in the wilderness, it had looked within itself, and, by heaven! I tell you, it had gone mad. I had—for my sins, I suppose—to go through the ordeal of looking into it myself" (145). The chaos Marlow sees within himself and what he fights against is hinted at indirectly in Marlow's summing up after Kurtz's death. Marlow's real plight (and Conrad's real fear), the passivity that Guerard points out, stems from a vacancy at the core of his being, an absence of instinctual vitality, a center of lifelessness tantamount to death. Irrupting into consciousness, this terrible emptiness, if unresisted, would result in the extinction of self. And because of this psychic deficiency, explaining in part Marlow's feeling that he is an impostor, no assured sense of autonomy is possible. Such a condition is described by Laing in *The Divided Self* as "primary ontological insecurity,"[7] the deep-seated anxiety in a person who never gained a sense of trust in his own separate identity, an individual with no inner confirmation of self. When the substantiality of one's very existence as a person is always called into question, no definite belief, no absolute value can be sustained because it is not fed by underlying supportive feelings.

Kurtz has forced Marlow to penetrate the underside of consciousness in that "inappreciable moment of time" when he stepped over "the threshold of the invisible." Kurtz's self-judgment, "The horror! The horror!" applies also to the dreadful nothingness within Marlow. "The most you can hope from it [life] is some knowledge of yourself," Marlow says.

> I have wrestled with death. It is the most unexciting contest you can
> imagine. It takes place in an impalpable grayness, with nothing un-
> derfoot, with nothing around, without spectators, without clamour,
> without glory, without the great desire of victory, without the great

> fear of defeat, in a sickly atmosphere of tepid scepticism, without much
> belief in your own right, and still less in that of your adversary.
> . . . .
> And it is not my own extremity I remember best—a vision of grayness
> without form filled with physical pain, and a careless contempt for the
> evanescence of all things—even of this pain itself. (148–49)

Had Marlow gone completely over the edge, he fears he would have
been buried just as Kurtz was buried. The extremity that is Marlow's
receives its ultimate expression in *Nostromo*'s Martin Decoud. A skep-
tic and nonbeliever, Decoud grapples with the same destructive inner
void during his prolonged isolation on the Great Isabel until his grasp
of his own reality disintegrates utterly, and he goes to an inexorable
suicide.

This sense of nonbeing overwhelms Marlow in a hopelessness but
a slight remove from suicide. Such apathy withers faith. "I was within
a hair's breadth of the last opportunity for pronouncement, and I
found with humiliation that probably I would have nothing to say"
(151). Marlow has no moral conviction to sustain him in his crisis. He
regards Kurtz's lucid cry as an "affirmation, a moral victory," because this assertion of conscience is an assertion of character and
belief. "He had summed up—he had judged. 'The horror!' He was
a remarkable man. After all, this was the expression of some sort of
belief; it had candour, it had conviction" (151). Kurtz has spoken for
Marlow. The implication of his words is that without the conscious
will to resist, a man is utterly lost, a stark truth which for Marlow is
an imperative for fortitude. Despite the terrible knowledge he pos-
sesses, despite the profound despair that strikes at the heart of his
existence, Marlow does not follow Kurtz to the grave. The necessity
of the man going forward in spite of the worst is a deeply personal
impulse in Conrad, whose own life was a prolonged ordeal of striving. Marlow has been pushed to the brink himself, and his suffering
is intensified because he shares sympathetically in Kurtz's own. For
Marlow, Kurtz's struggle and death is a vicarious sacrifice that necessarily deepens his allegiance. And it is loyalty to Kurtz which provides the impetus and purpose for Marlow's going on and eventually
affords new meaning to his life.

The dying Kurtz entrusts Marlow with his personal effects, ex-
tending a bond begun when Marlow pledged to the Russian to safe-

guard his master's reputation. By preventing the Company from exploiting Kurtz posthumously, Marlow disassociates himself firmly from their corrupting contact. He refuses the manager access to Kurtz's private papers and, back in Brussels, rebuffs the Company official scrounging for profitable documents. Marlow presents family letters and memoranda to the senile and sentimental cousin, who totters off with his belief in the universal genius of his relative unmarred. To Kurtz's journalist colleague, Marlow offers for publication the "Suppression" report, postscript torn off, and so preserves Kurtz's missionary image for the public. But Marlow's personal anguish is unmitigated. His temperature is seldom normal during this time, but his aunt's conventional health remedies are unavailing. "It was not my strength that wanted nursing, it was my imagination that wanted soothing" (152). In the spiritual malaise that continues to afflict him, Marlow is still haunted by the dead man. In an attempt to exorcise that memory, he brings to the Intended the remaining letters and her portrait. Marlow gallantly spares her the shattering revelation of Kurtz's final words, and the lie keeps intact her spiritualized conception. Homage to that ideal gives her life its fundamental meaning. Despite its illusoriness, the ideal is essential because it is protective and sustaining. At the same time Marlow's commitment to this lie suggests that a vital illusion has ended for him: his romantic conception of the heroic man of action. Marlow could have been inspired by that fiction before the Congo, and perhaps he harbored such a conception about himself, about the redemptive possibilities of action, a faith projected onto his imagined view of Kurtz before they met. That no such man exists is driven home by Kurtz's example. And what ends for Marlow is the possibility of forging for himself a new future or gaining a renewed sense of his future through emulation of the great man, the large figure of daring and energy.[8] Marlow's lie to the woman implies that he is no longer liable to idealize himself or other men in that way. Depressed and demoralized as he is, Marlow, like the Intended, is in need of a saving illusion.

Previously, Marlow had declared his loathing of the lie, which in the context of his conversation with a white agent relates to a sham identity, a distorted image of himself fabricated by others.

> You know I hate, detest, and can't bear a lie, not because I am straighter than the rest of us, but simply because it appals me. There is a taint

of death, a flavour of mortality in lies—which is exactly what I hate
and detest in the world—what I want to forget. It makes me miserable
and sick, like biting something rotten would do. Temperament, I suppose. Well, I went near enough to it by letting the young fool there
believe anything he liked to imagine as to my influence in Europe. I
became in an instant as much of a pretence as the rest of the bewitched
pilgrims. (82)

The spurious self is necessarily hateful, and Marlow admits to living
a lie about himself. But his words reverberate with deeper meaning.
His physical revulsion, tantamount to self-disgust, suggests a reaction
against not only the imposed counterfeit self, but against some "taint
of death" within, something corrupt and deficient in his essential nature which he senses dimly but cannot acknowledge. What Marlow
hates and wants to forget is the hollowness he fears in himself and
must suppress. When he peers into his soul in the Congo, he describes this ultimate self-confrontation as his having "wrestled with
death." Psychic conflict is so violent as to sever his sources of faith.
Just as the Intended would be crushed by learning that Kurtz was
an impostor, her image of him fallacious, Marlow cannot live mean-
ingfully if he submits completely to the undeniable feeling that he is
an impostor. The truth is that Marlow's sense of identity will always
be illusory, uncertain, and incomplete; any ideal self-conception will
be felt to be partially a lie. But to be without any belief, without any
vital image of self, is unendurable. Marlow is regenerated through
his bond with Kurtz, and his saving illusion is to be transformed into
an image of Kurtz, to become a voice whose task is to tell the story.
   Marlow's quest for identity leads to self-renewal, and this theme is
bound up intimately with Conrad's use of character doubles. Most
evident in the Marlow-Kurtz relationship, this technique is apparent
also in Marlow's brief association with the Russian harlequin, the romantic wanderer now an ardent hero-worshiper of Kurtz. Points of
kinship between Marlow and the twenty-five year old hint at a special
identification. Marlow is also a wanderer, unrepresentative of the
maritime profession, and the young sailor addresses Marlow as a
"brother seaman." In less extreme form, the fledgling's "unreflecting
audacity" and utter thoughtlessness of self are qualities found in
Marlow, the recklessness and self-ignorance implicit in the Britisher's
venture to Africa. This figure in motley seems to incarnate the
"glamour of youth," a romanticism also part of Marlow's character.

Commenting on his explorer's impulse to his companions on the *Nellie*, Marlow confesses to having at one time been seduced by the glamor of place. But now, he says, "the glamour's off" (52). The book on seamanship Marlow finds and returns to its Russian owner is a more direct link between the two. Their mutual attachment to the volume and the value they place on it point up a callowness and lack of penetration common to each. Both men are inexplicably in Africa, drawn to Kurtz, and impressed by the man's eloquence. But the crucial factor uniting them is their abiding fidelity to Kurtz, and Marlow fulfills more perfectly than he anticipated the adherent's earnest request to preserve Kurtz's public name.

The highly personal nature of "Heart of Darkness" reveals itself further in this double relationship between the two seamen. Marlow's sympathetic identification with the fellow seems to be Conrad's own. In its force and sustained feeling, Marlow's encomium to this apprentice version of himself (beginning Chapter 3) implies the author speaking directly, the tone of wonder and admiration suggesting an older Conrad addressing a representation of his own improbable youth. Numerous autobiographical parallels exist. The disciple's Russian nationality corresponds with Conrad's original status.[9] The harlequin's father is an archpriest (Lord Jim has a parson father), a detail which suggests the mystical religiosity Conrad's father Apollo Korzeniowski developed after his wife's death. The sketch of the youth's background reads like a thinly disguised outline of Conrad's own taking to sea. Marlow learns that the fellow "had run away from school, had gone to sea in a Russian ship; ran away again; served some time in English ships; was now reconciled with the archpriest. He made a point of that " (123).

As the patched-up Russian adventurer bids good-bye, he asks for and Marlow gives him a pair of old shoes. Shoes have already been associated with the theme of identity, Marlow stepping into Fresleven's shoes. Marlow had discarded those—symbolically, a shedding of the pseudoself—before actually meeting Kurtz. Now, Marlow provides the departing harlequin with replacement shoes. This gift and farewell scene suggest Conrad taking affectionate leave of a younger self and a phase of his life, and the exchange between the two men heralds Marlow's gradual development of another identity. In relinquishing his dying patient to Marlow, the anonymous guardian places in Marlow's hands the care of Kurtz's reputation. What begins for Marlow as a transferred obligation of loyalty grows into the deepest of attachments. Marlow will also proclaim Kurtz a remarkable man and, again like his younger double, become a disciple. But so profoundly is Marlow linked to Kurtz, perhaps by "an impulse of unconscious loyalty, or the fulfilment of one of those ironic necessities that lurk in the facts of human existence" (155), that in trying to extricate himself from Kurtz, he in a sense becomes Kurtz. Marlow replaces the master by symbolically merging with him. Kurtz's voice is extinguished but Marlow becomes a voice. Marlow's pose of a meditating Buddha (at the beginning of "Heart of Darkness" but some time after the Congo experience) recalls Kurtz's image of a bald idol discoursing. Kurtz has provided Marlow with a necessity to tell the tale, to reflect upon its meaning, and in the process to grow in self-awareness and moral consciousness, values and concerns associated more with the novelist than the sailor. In effect, the Congo experience culminating with Kurtz has made Marlow a serious storyteller, and in that development lies his renewal. A vital realization of identity has occurred, not a "stepping into someone else's shoes" but a merging that embodies emotional and spiritual connections. Literally and symbolically, "Heart of Darkness" marks Conrad's efflorescence as a distinguished writer, inaugurating his major phase as a novelist even as it unfolds the transformation of seaman to storyteller.

One of the tale's unavoidable conclusions is that no informing moral idea can justify the lust for aggrandizement in the individual or in nations; the egotism of Kurtz and the imperialism of Europe, both idealized in the name of spiritual progress, are irredeemable. The conventional appearance of society and human action, its apparent rationality, meaning, and moral intention, belies a hollow center, an intrinsic corruption and destructive potential. No absolutes can be sustained and all things are possible. What protects one from these terrible truths are repression, illusions, and lies. Marlow returns to the sepulchral city of Brussels initiated into a Dostoevskian universe. Out of the heartsickening sense of failure and disillusionment emerges an enlargement of consciousness, an inescapable tragic burden for Conrad and his art.

CHAPTER THREE

Lord Jim: Romantic Retreat

I

DEVOTION to duty is the one inviolable law of the seaman. Working against egotism and the claims of selfhood, the maritime code, while allowing for a degree of initiative, must guard against uniqueness and individual aberration. Absolute obedience to this standard is embodied in the two *Patna* helmsmen, nonwhite and unintellectual, who stood unswervingly at their station. Lack of imagination and unquestioning fidelity saved both from possible panic. One, at the inquiry, said he thought nothing of his action at the time. The other "explained that he had a knowledge of some evil thing befalling the ship, but there had been no order; he could not remember an order; why should he leave the helm?"[1] This man is a "damning witness" to a Jim who did not even recall his presence. Another vindicator of the code is the French lieutenant of the rescuing vessel. Because he deemed it proper, he remained aboard the crippled steamer with its threatening bulkhead for thirty hours while two quartermasters on the *Réunion* were stationed with axes ready to cut the tow line. He sees matters exactly as they are and acts upon them almost thoughtlessly. Their actions partake of the heroism which Jim dreams for himself, but these seamen regard their conduct as the expected fulfillment of service. Certainly, Conrad respects these men and what they represent. Jim, however, is incapable of the steersmen's utter self-subordination or of the French lieutenant's composed and efficient assertion in the performance of duty.

Foiling the trio that answered their obligation is the renegade white crew—"three dirty owls." Before the trial, the chief engineer goes mad, a curious case of D.T.'s; his reptilian hallucination in the hospital is analogous to Jim's images of panic. The second culprit is confined to a hospital bed, arms splintered, quite light-headed. Two no-accounts, concludes Marlow, nobodies, beyond awareness and hence outside moral accountability. The German skipper bolts from the official condemnation in a ramshackle gharry. "Take away my certificate," he sneers. "Take it. I don't want the certificate. . . . I shpit on it" (42). Moral comment is implied in his physical description, and Conrad emphasizes that he does not belong to the fellowship of the craft or to the responsible human community deserving of our concern. "There was something obscene in the sight of his naked flesh. His bared breast glistened soft and greasy as though he had sweated out his fat in his sleep. . . . the odious and fleshy figure . . . fixed itself in his [Jim's] memory for ever as the incarnation of everything vile and base that lurks in the world we love" (21). Such antithetical characters, the steadfast and the faithless, present no conflict for our allegiance.

But Jim is problematic, one of us: in decency and moral intention, in responsible English background, in appearance and intensity of feeling, in his human limitations. His one fatal act speaks for all of us who have turned our backs on others or failed in one way or another. Appealing instinctively to Marlow, Jim seems to personify good faith and honesty, seems to renew belief in humanity; his youth seems to hold rich promise for the future. But if the immorality of the German captain is glaringly obvious, Jim's fairness is misleading. Unable to reconcile semblance with facts, Marlow suspects Jim's more than criminal weakness, more because of its deceptive and internal quality. "The commonest sort of fortitude prevents us from becoming criminals in a legal sense; it is from weakness unknown, but perhaps suspected . . . from weakness that may lie hidden, watched or unwatched, prayed against or manfully scorned, repressed or maybe ignored more than half a lifetime, not one of us is safe" (42–43).

Though all men are potential lawbreakers, only some of the apparently upright are exposed, and the agonizing question is how Jim, so seemingly wholesome, could be unsound. "I would have trusted the deck to that youngster on the strength of a single glance, and gone to sleep with both eyes—and, by Jove! it wouldn't have been safe. There are depths of horror in that thought" (45).

Insinuating itself into Marlow's imagination, Jim's plight moves him to search for some form of exoneration, "some profound and redeeming cause" that would exorcise "the doubt of the sovereign power enthroned in a fixed standard of conduct" and justify his concern for Jim. Such doubt imperils Marlow's own moral foundation as a member of the profession; it hints at the dread of nihilism. What if the code is too narrow and dogmatic, if it does not encompass a broad or complex enough range of experience, making insufficient allowance for extreme situations and psychic failings? Marlow's personal interest is based most deeply on sympathetic identification:

> Was it for my own sake that I wished to find some shadow of an excuse for that young fellow whom I had never seen before, but whose appearance alone added a touch of personal concern to the thoughts suggested by the knowledge of his weakness—made it a thing of mystery and terror—like a hint of a destructive fate ready for us all whose youth—in its day—had resembled his youth? I fear that such was the secret motive of my prying. (51)

According to Guerard, "He is loyal to Jim as one must be to another or potential self, to the criminally weak self that may still exist."[2]

At the same time, Jim embodies for Marlow a vital image of youthful energy and aspiration that touches unconscious sources of his own faith. Though Marlow investigates and tests an absolute standard of conduct, its necessity and rigorous terms are not seriously threatened in his mind. What appears to be at stake rather is the poignant need to reaffirm his belief in the possibilities of human effort, in the sense that something ennobling and uplifting may be won in a world that seems to darken any apparent success. Conrad is also deeply attached to the impulse of striving forward, especially in the man who has failed. Zabel observes that in Marlow "disillusionment must still compete with an invincible curiosity and a tenacious confidence in the capacity of men to justify their survival in a world of baffling or destructive forces."[3] Hanging over Jim is the specter of futurelessness. Even if Jim is not, Marlow is assailed by a burden of finality at the trial. "These proceedings had all the cold vengefulness of a death-sentence, had all the cruelty of a sentence of exile" (158). Afterward, Marlow fears that Jim will decline in pathetic and shabby ways, stumble into a dead-end obscurity or worse. Though Marlow suffers empathetically—he identifies unself-pityingly his earlier self with Jim's endangered youth—this dread of poverty and an undistinguished life assumes a fierce potency in Nostromo and Razumov. The confidant/ally's need for the other self, the young wrongdoer, to come through in the face of exile and desolation receives a sharper focus and an intense dramatic realization in "The Secret Sharer," where the captain's spiritual wholeness depends upon Leggatt's moving confidently into the future. The concentrated skepticism and unrelieved tragic power of "Heart of Darkness" are lessened in *Lord Jim*, so that the novel may be considered a retreat from the bleak pessimism of the African story.[4] Although Marlow's reflections and doubts about Jim deepen, Conrad keeps the narrator from the black pit of nihilism that his namesake experiences in "Heart of Darkness." One notes that Jim's fate does not bring Marlow to despair.

Though intention, to some degree, distinguishes Jim from the others, he deserted also, and the act declares his mutual guilt. "The examination of the only man able and willing to face it [the inquiry] was beating futilely round the well-known fact, and the play of questions upon it was as instructive as the tapping with a hammer on an iron box, were the object to find out what's inside" (56). "They wanted facts. Facts! They demanded facts from him, as if facts could explain anything" (29)! Conrad's art, of course, reaches beyond the mere enumeration of facts, to their context, meaning, and suggestiveness. Marlow sees at once that what counts about Jim's story is that which cannot be reduced to facts. He distrusts them as Conrad mistrusts direct chronology. Both factuality and a progressive time sequence suggest simplicity, which is oversimplification, present a reality clearly decipherable and capable of being mastered, and avoid the elusiveness and intricate density that is closer to Conrad's sense of truth. In the infinity of human behavior, there is a frightfully complex moral reality that defies ethical formulation and eludes the certainty of definition. One way Conrad involves us in this ambiguity is by permit-

ting us to believe that the *Patna* went under, its masthead light drop-
ping "like a lighted match you throw down." Not until the trial is
well under way do we receive an explanation as to why the ship's
masthead lamp vanished, causing the semblance of foundering. If
reality so easily becomes illusion, if appearance so readily lends itself
to self-serving interpretation, how can moral certitude be established?

Jim's failure in the rescue operation aboard a training craft prefigures his conduct during the *Patna* emergency. Making many voy-
ages and becoming thoroughly knowledgeable of his duties, Jim then
becomes first mate of a fine ship, "without ever having been tested
by those events of the sea that show in the light of day the inner
worth of a man, the edge of his temper, and the fibre of his stuff;
that reveal the quality of his resistance and the secret truth of his
pretences, not only to others but also to himself" (10). During a violent gale, one whose elemental ferocity impresses him with a "purpose of malice," Jim is disabled by a falling spar, and when the ship
docks at an Eastern port, he enters a hospital to convalesce. This
accident, naturalistic in itself, suggests also a lameness of character.
Fellow patients like himself "had now a horror of the home service,
with its harder conditions, severer view of duty, and the hazard of
stormy oceans. They were attuned to the eternal peace of Eastern
sky and sea" (13). Thus, the East woos Jim, appeals irresistibly to his
romantic temperament, promises a refuge for hidden fears. It is directly after his hospital stay with these men who have a soft spot,
men determined "to lounge safely through existence," that Jim signs
as chief mate of the *Patna*. Dorothy Van Ghent questions whether
Jim's selection of the *Patna* is designed to protect his dream from
reality.[5] Yes, Jim is contriving to win heroic achievement on his own
terms; by choosing an easier passage in seas apparently more hos-
pitable, Jim is trying to avoid the unpredictable and malicious in nature and soothe his fears. Less exacting duty will allow for long spells
of solitary reverie and will not curb initiative when daring action is
needed. Dreamy self-absorption dulls further Jim's weak critical sense.
On the *Patna* deck musing about the crew members, Jim winces at
the sight of the repulsive German, "but he was too pleasurably lan-
guid to dislike actively this or any other thing. . . . The line dividing his meditation from a surreptitious doze on his feet was thinner
than a thread in a spider's web" (24–25).

Jim's romanticism is inseparable from a callowness of character, and for Conrad these qualities make consciousness and its implied self-knowledge unattainable. The question arises whether callowness is willful ignorance or "innocent" unawareness, innocuous in the sense that moral understanding is beyond the individual given his nature? Neither mentor nor experience has instructed Jim in life's deeper meanings, and considering the absolute necessity of his illusions, his stubbornness, and lack of intellect, one doubts whether Jim can learn in any substantial way. How much a mitigating factor is callowness, then, in assessing moral, as opposed to legal, accountability? That Jim failed to recognize or did not give sufficient weight to the substandard condition of the *Patna* (the inquiry determined that the ship was unfit and unseaworthy), to the suspect nature of the crew, and to the overcrowding and safety hazard, is to say he is morally obtuse and not a first-rate seaman. Though Jim is a competent worker, he lacks a good officer's discrimination. Marlow or Brierly would never sail on a *Patna*. Jim's carelessness in joining the pilgrim ship, though more marked, resembles Marlow's willingness in "Heart of Darkness" to work for an exploitative company because of his own romantic desire to reach the Congo. Such callowness can have enormous consequences, and in a person of grown years it amounts to irresponsibility, denies him moral stature. The court's verdict of guilty of dereliction and the punishment of debarment from the service point up the professional seaman aspect of Conrad's judgment.[6] It reveals further Conrad's deeper interest in the effects of crime and exile on a sympathetic character, especially the man's efforts to deny an imposed public definition, whose effect is to categorize and so shrink identity.

Jim comes to the *Patna* untried, ignorant of himself, vulnerable in his callowness, and lulled into a false security of his own making. Self-deceived into the illusion of a beneficent universe, Jim, on the *Patna*'s bridge, is "penetrated by the great certitude of unbounded safety and peace that could be read on the silent aspect of nature" (17). A hint of the impending danger is foreshadowed when he glances idly at the ship's navigational chart and measuring instruments—"the pencil with its sharp end touching the Somali coast lay round and still like a naked ship's spar floating in the pool of a sheltered dock" (20). The submerged derelict hitting the *Patna* indicates both the

menacing, the dangerously unpredictable in life and the threat of
the unconscious. Paralleling the deceptive calm of the water is Jim's
surface serenity; the unexpected object striking from below suggests
the eruption of the irrational, here instinctive fear. Although he does
act during the crisis—checking the damaged bulkhead, getting his
water bottle for a pilgrim, cutting the lifeboats free—when effective
action is crucial, Jim can do nothing, made passive by his panic-evok-
ing imagination. His "swift and forestalling vision" had "turned him
into cold stone from the soles of his feet to the nape of his neck; but
there was a hot dance of thoughts in his head, a dance of lame, blind,
mute thoughts—a whirl of awful cripples" (96–97).

Unable to grasp a situation and its possibilities, Jim becomes trapped
by an inflexibility stemming from his misperceptions and egotism.
His imagination is given to melodramatic distortion that intensifies
his fear.[7] For his daydream heroism to be glorious, the dangers must
be extreme. Having immersed himself in adolescent fantasies of disaster and escape, when the actual crisis does occur, he is susceptible
to drawing the worst possible conclusions. And because he feels compelled to deal with the emergency single-handedly (the pilgrims are
obstacles rather than potential helpers to him) and hence must fail,
he succumbs quickly to a sense of impotence and hopelessness. Jim
leaps because of fear but also out of a feeling of helplessness, a conviction that nothing can be done. Certainly, Conrad convinces us that
the external threat is real and formidable (a means also of gaining
empathy for Jim)—ship's list, deserting crew, straining bulkhead, approaching squall—but it must be remembered that we receive these
details through Jim's eyes. In fact, the bulkhead did hold, the pilgrims did not rampage, "the sea never got up that night to any extent" (112). To the unanswerable question of what he would have
done that Jim throws at Marlow and is forced upon the reader, Conrad
provides the character and example of the French lieutenant, a man
of clear-sightedness, discipline, and willed courage. One knows that
he would not have panicked. If he were the only officer remaining
on board, one can imagine him enlisting the aid of pilgrims in performing emergency measures, organizing pumping duties, and
maintaining order. But Jim, with his superiority and one ambition
to be a hero, is loathe to ask for assistance.

The scene on the *Patna* is grotesquely ironic in its contrasts: three crewmen in a frenzy of movement struggling to liberate a jammed lifeboat, hundreds of unsuspecting Moslems, the acting third mate lying dead of heart failure, two Malays standing dutifully by the wheel, and Jim frozen to paralysis. Poised on the ship's edge, helpless before the onslaught of imagination, ears pelted by shouts to a dead man, brushed by the vanguard of a squall, "I had jumped. . . . It seems."

By nature, Jim cannot reconcile his deed with his self-image; how he conceives of the entire *Patna* experience is necessarily protective and self-serving. He appears voluntarily at the inquiry not primarily out of a sense of guilt but because of a stubborn pride, as if he must demonstrate that he can take this public exposure and punishment without flinching, insisting to himself that the act does not identify him, that he is capable of saving a *Patna*. Psychologist Gordon Allport regards guilt as a "poignant suffering . . . a sense of violated value, a disgust at falling short of the ideal self-image."[8] Wanting adventure and glory, Jim could never be satisfied with the prosaic and monotonous tenor of sea life. Guilt is highly personalized, and because he aspires to be a hero and not a good officer, because the only reward of the sea must elude him, "the perfect love of work," his factual violation of the maritime code does not arouse conscious guilt feelings on that score. He feels disgraced, a loss of honor, certainly sharp regret for a missed opportunity, but he seems fearful of accepting guilt, which would mean an admission of cowardice. He never acknowledges personal responsibility. Desperately, he maintains that something external and extenuating was the cause—the "villainy of circumstance" or the malignancy of nature. Marlow observes that "he made so much of his disgrace while it is the guilt alone that matters" (77). "He is romantic," says Stein.

> And because you not always can keep your eyes shut there comes the real trouble—the heart pain—the world pain. . . . it is not good for you to find you cannot make your dream come true, for the reason that you not strong enough are, or not clever enough. . . . And all the time you are such a fine fellow, too! (213)

As a character, Jim could not survive the loss of ego-ideal and attendant psychic dissolution and despair that Marlow suffered in "Heart of Darkness." Jim's illusion of self is crucially necessary to sustain and motivate him. Marlow's analysis appreciates Jim's fine sensibilities—

"a sort of sublimated, idealised selfishness. . . . A little coarser nature would not have borne the strain; it would have had to come to
terms with itself—with a sigh, with a grunt, or even with a guffaw;
a still coarser one would have remained invulnerably ignorant and
completely uninteresting" (177). Conrad must keep Jim romantic and
deserving of our concern even while that romanticism shields him
from consciousness.

                                    II

DESPITE Jim's simplicity and intellectual limitations, Conrad forces
the reader not to dismiss him as "immature," neurotic, or morbidly
sensitive. One effect of Conrad's use of multiple perspectives, an
expression of his "extreme ethical scrupulosity,"[9] is to compel a growing
appreciation of Jim's particular response to his dilemma even though
it entails continued suffering and seems to admit of no solution. The
various characters who comment on Jim by the same token reveal
something of themselves. While each voice in this choral structure
adds its validity to the expanding complexity of Jim and his case,
each speaker's personality and life situation qualify what is said. To
assess these viewpoints separately and as they play off against each
other is to be driven to realize that the novel seeks to perpetuate the
anxiety of uncertainty. It works to thwart any attempt to formulate
and retain an assured judgment of Jim. Here, I would suggest, is an
instance of Conrad keeping a character at a safe distance from his
penetrating intelligence. By refracting his complex attitude toward
Jim in different perspectives and by using Marlow as a surrogate to
combine sympathy and criticism, Conrad diffuses his own moral
judgment of Jim, which is absorbed by his art.

    Brierly is a seemingly immaculate representative of the service. "He
had never in his life made a mistake, never had an accident, never
a mishap, never a check in his steady rise, and he seemed to be one
of those lucky fellows who know nothing of indecision, much less of
self-mistrust" (57). But what Jim means to Brierly is probably the
very things of which he has remained ignorant or that he has chosen
to exclude from his range of experience. The man's anger at Jim
goes deeper than disgrace to the service, behavior unbefitting profes-

sional decency in eating all that dirt. When he even suggests to Marlow an offer of flight money to the accused, it is a desperate measure at self-protection. Jim represents one of those disturbing possibilities which poisons one's confidence, eats away at those few simple notions that constitute a man's moral foundation. He inspired, thinks Marlow, "one of those trifles that awaken ideas—start into life some thought with which a man unused to such a companionship finds it impossible to live" (59). The *Patna* episode is appalling enough to snap the mind of the ship's chief engineer, veteran of twenty-four years in the tropics, a consequence which helps convince us that Jim can personalize the affair for Brierly and drive him to his own leap. The missing four iron belaying pins that Jones supposes Brierly put in his pockets as dead weight suggest a meticulous determination to succeed in suicide, a measure that reveals how deeply stricken is his will to live. (Conrad repeats this detail in *Nostromo* when Decoud pockets four silver ingots so that his body will sink in the gulf after he shoots himself.) Jones remarks that once over the side, Brierly "did not try to swim a stroke, the same as he would have had pluck enough to keep up all day long on the bare chance had he fallen overboard accidently" (62). Brierly lacks the fiber of Leggatt, the proud swimmer, and Jim has Conrad's admiration in his dogged resistance to surrender, in his going on despite a blighted future.

Brierly's suicide is a perfect reflection of the professionalism he lived. He passes out of the world without melodrama, quietly, efficiently, with his affairs well-ordered. He is scrupulous to the point of laying the correct course, providing detailed instructions, and insuring that his dog will not jump after him. Brierly believes his reputation and its influence will be undiminished after his death. Suicide, he seems to think, is solely a private matter. But like Jim's leap, once this act is known to others, it assumes a meaning and status independent of the actor's subjective determination. Brierly's exalted self-regard is evident in his suicide, which prefigures and comments upon Jim's death. In his letter to the owners, he affirms that even now he is not betraying their confidence in him since he is leaving command to the competent Mr. Jones. However, the company disregards his recommendation for a successor. The world, obviously, does not revere Brierly as he idolized himself. In the image of disconsolate old Jones commemorating his former captain aboard the squalid *Fire-Queen* and watching over the sorrowing Rover, a "veil of inexpressibly mean pathos" is thrown over Brierly's remembered figure. "Who can tell," muses Marlow, "what flattering view he had induced himself to take of his own suicide" (64)? Outside the closed terms of Brierly's own egotism, Conrad shows how short-lived is his splendor, how shabby his posthumous treatment by fate. When it comes to Jim's death, Conrad must elevate his protagonist even while he presents this final act so that Jim's heroic claims do not go unopposed, neither giving too much weight to Jim's view of himself nor allowing "fate," as in Brierly's case, to press down too firmly so as to rob him completely of the stature he thinks is his.

A second professional, the elderly French lieutenant, who considers bravery a matter-of-fact condition of the service, offers another perspective. His interview with Marlow, three years after the court of inquiry but juxtaposed with Jim's vivid retelling to Marlow of the *Patna* episode, serves to check the growing sympathy Jim elicits from Marlow and the reader by presenting a man who has measured up to the situation that both Jim and Brierly found intolerable. The lieutenant has achieved numerous triumphs, but in contrast to his English counterpart Brierly, he is unmindful of reputation. A gunshot scar and old sabre wound suggest other encounters with death and a career not at all prosaic. Tolerant, at ease with himself, possessed of wide sympathies and an incisive mind, he is unburdened by the enslavement to ego-ideal that links Jim and Brierly. He hints that once he experienced fear, but one can live with that knowledge, he says, and clearly he was unimpaired thereafter. Conrad pays high tribute to this man etched by experience, whose conduct during the *Patna* rescue adds moral authority to his words. Compared with a peasant priest in his impassivity and "appearance of devout concentration," he recalls the Buddha image of the reflective Marlow in "Heart of Darkness." He sympathizes with Jim, but one does not die of being afraid, he says. "Given a certain combination of circumstances, fear is sure to come. . . . And even for those who do not believe this truth there is fear all the same—the fear of themselves. . . . Man is born a coward. . . . But habit—habit—necessity . . . the eye of others. . . . One puts up with it. And then the example of others who are no better than yourself, and yet make good countenance" (146–47). To Marlow's comment that he is taking a lenient view, the Frenchman demurs:

> I contended that one may get on knowing very well that one's courage does not come of itself. . . . There's nothing much in that to get upset about. One truth the more ought not to make life impossible. . . . But the honour—the honour, monsieur! . . . that is real—that is! And what life may be worth when . . . the honour is gone . . . I can offer no opinion—because—monsieur—I know nothing of it. (148)

The lieutenant's reputation and self-respect have never been compromised, and his astuteness extends only to the limit of his own experience. In Marlow's disappointment at this just qualification lies Conrad's implication that no definitive response to Jim is possible. Now, when the narrative moves back in time to the trial, we are more ready to accept the rightness of the expected verdict. But because Jim refuses escape money and insists on seeing it through, an act which severs him morally from the other deserters and bespeaks a gritty pride, Conrad solidifies our concern for Jim and redirects the focus of interest to his future, to the prospect of what will happen to a twenty-three year old on the run with absolutely nowhere to go. Conrad is thus preparing the ground for the open, adventurous Patusan section of the novel.

The sequence involving Chester and Robinson, an absurd and fantastic tandem, contains some fine touches. Well-traveled and many-jobbed Chester (a gross intimation of what Jim might become), debased adventurer, a vagabond and man of quick profit schemes, scoffs that Jim takes it to heart. What's all the to-do over a bit of ass's skin, he wonders, echoing the *Patna*'s German skipper. "You must see things exactly as they are—if you don't, you may just as well give in at once. You will never do anything in this world" (162), Chester exclaims, oblivious to his own want of accomplishment. Chester would like Jim, whom he recognizes accurately "is no earthly good for anything" now in the workaday world, to manage his uninhabitable guano island, two six-shooters in his belt, "supreme boss over coolies." Although this picture of Jim is repulsive to Marlow, Chester's vulgar conception foreshadows as grotesque parody Jim as lord of Patusan, and it does suggest the adolescent quality of Jim's dreams of glory that is part of the soft core of his romanticism. Appropriately, Chester's crony is the notorious Old Robinson, rumored to have resorted to cannibalism in a desperate situation but worthy in Chester's eyes because he ignored public vilification, not taking it to heart. He saw things

as they were and survived. With Robinson's funds Chester buys a
beat-up tramp steamer whose inferiority recalls the *Patna*. However,
with his partner enfeebled and his guano scheme outlandish and
dangerously impractical, Chester's rigorous pragmatism is mocked
by implication. Even these two have their illusions. And Jim, stripped
of his certificate and hope for a glamorous future, is like Old Robinson in being "useless," in having to be led by Marlow as Chester
leads his drooping, senile companion. As coda, Conrad adds that
Chester and crew vanished en route to Walpole islet, presumed lost
during a hurricane.

Another opinion of Jim is delivered by Cornelius, the abject and
defeated Malacca Portuguese of Patusan, fictional descendant of
Almayer and the rotting outcast Willems. By temperament antipa-
thetic to Jim, Cornelius lacks the active force to destroy this young
usurper whom he hates. For such an assault his insidiousness must
ally itself with the malevolent will of Brown. Though the sycophan-
tic, aggrieved, and envious Cornelius, childish himself, is hardly a
formidable judge of character, one must not dismiss his spiteful description of Jim: "He is a fool. A little child." Immaturity is seen in
Jim's selfishness and inflexibility, in his exalted and reckless belief in
his own personal power, in his overscrupulous regard for maintaining his knight's image of purity. Jim tries to be more than human.
And it is Cornelius's grasp of Jim's naiveté that helps bring about his
downfall. Despising the Englishman for his confidence, decency, and
uncalculating nature, for being above pettiness and temptation, he
knows that Jim is vulnerable to treachery under the guise of fair
play.

Of all the satellite characters who reflect and comment on aspects
of Jim, Stein shares the fullest kinship with him. In offering a practical remedy in the form of a romantic opportunity—Patusan as a
refuge at the cost of danger—Stein is passing on to Jim the help he
had received earlier from an elder Scotsman who had in effect adopted
him. Jim's second chance enables him to relive Stein's adventurous
past. Escaping from his native Bavaria at twenty-two because of his
revolutionary activities, a youthful hero of innumerable exploits in
the interior of Celebes, Stein has an immediate affinity with and understanding of Jim's type. Like the French officer, he has a courage
which is unselfconscious, a quality of steadiness in doing what one

must under extreme hazard. Thwarting an assassination attempt on him and killing three attackers at close range, Stein reveals excitement only at capturing a rare butterfly directly afterward. In its forgetfulness of danger for personal pleasure, this reaction resembles the Frenchman's annoyance at missing his mealtime wine aboard the stricken *Patna*. To these unmelodramatic men, their bravery is nothing out of the ordinary, and they do not see heroism as the occasion for glory and self-congratulation.[10] That both also possess penetrating minds suggests how highly Conrad values the integration of the active and intellectual in one man.

Stein's encomium to the butterfly—"this masterpiece of Nature—the great artist"—is richly metaphoric and contains one of Conrad's rare fictional tributes to art. Jim's ideal self-conception, perfect in imagination, resembles the butterfly in its splendor and fragility. Before it is claimed by decay (Stein secured his beauty while it was sitting on a small heap of dirt), the butterfly is sealed in glass, frozen and imperishable. Similarly, Conrad's art captures and preserves a vision of Jim's reality which is elusive and intricate. (In the Preface to "The Nigger of the *Narcissus*" appear these words on the task of the artist: "To snatch in a moment of courage, from the remorseless rush of time, a passing phase of life.") Like the collector's unspoiled prize, Jim dies in the fullness of youth, unmarked by time and experience; he is spared the knowledge with which Stein lives. Victorious over his enemy, happy with wife and daughter, Stein achieves his desires only at the moment he captures his long-sought specimen. But abruptly his world collapses with the murder of his friend Mohammed and the sudden deaths of wife and child. Though his tone often has the accent of pensive melancholy, Stein is not morbidly nostalgic or paralyzed by brooding. Shattered by the loss of family, he leaves the jungle to start afresh and amasses a fortune. It is too much to say that Stein is the successful version of Jim. He is significantly different from Jim in being guiltless of betrayal, in being free of the excesses of egotism, and in possessing intellectual capacity. His life testifies to the possibility that by holding fast to one's dream, one can endure on honorable terms despite exile and great personal misfortune.

One can say further that, in the context of the novel, Stein functions as the representation of the mature romantic, who embodies

Conrad's impulse of withdrawal into meditation. But Stein cannot
support too large a burden of Conrad's thought. Specifically, two
problems crucial to Conrad's developing conception of integrity, self-
affirmation and guilt, conflict radically with those elements of his
vision and temperament which point inescapably to withdrawal from
the world of action. Though this retreat may suggest the pursuit of
art (e.g., Stein and his butterflies, Marlow of "Heart of Darkness"
and his storytelling), Conrad could not formulate an imaginative resolution to these deepest concerns in the figure of the artist.[11] Stein's
reflections on man's innate restlessness, on man's propensity for self-
idealization that blinds him to the dual character of his impulses,
imply that by nature man cannot realize his dreams. Sensitized by
experience to the impermanence of things and life's unavoidable pain,
aware of the crippling effects of disillusionment, Stein appreciates
deeply the necessity of following one's dream, submitting to "the destructive element" of one's ideal. Although typical Conradian effects
of light and dark imagery cast doubt on the finality of Stein's utter-
ances, his romantic prescription is suited perfectly to the wholly romantic Jim, who is unable to forget or adapt, arrested by a failure
he cannot face.

III

PATUSAN is Jim's territory, remote from European contact, capable
of being transformed by a strong man with vision and purpose. Jim
exceeds all those projections for his future foreseen by the prudent,
worldly, or cynical. Marlow had confessed to doubts, and even Stein
is amazed at Jim's brilliant, imaginative success. Everyone saw him
going under or at best attaining a modest if mediocre recovery. In
part, it is this sense of overreaching all expectation that informs
Marlow's affirmation that Jim had achieved greatness. Spillover from
"Heart of Darkness" is evident when Conrad associates Jim with the
heroic spirit found in the early seventeenth-century English and Dutch
explorers and traders, a spirit which Conrad always cherished, the
pioneers and frontier-breakers "pushing out into the unknown in
obedience to an inward voice, to an impulse beating in the blood, to
a dream of the future" (227). In his quest for rehabilitation, Jim moves

beyond personal concerns, embracing the fate of the community as both leader and civilizing agent. But Conrad strains for effect in trying to magnify Jim as a carrier of Western order and justice. Jim is too limited a character for the role, and the tragic and compelling treatment of this civilizing endeavor in "Heart of Darkness" played out the jungle phase of this theme. Conrad's energies point to the need for a Costaguana, the half-wild, developing South American country that will come to life in *Nostromo*.

Fidelity, courage, and justice form the basis for Jim's supremacy in the island wilderness. He leads the people to victory in war, arbitrates their differences, earns their friendship. Among the populace, he grows famous and respected, his confidence apparently restored. Most important to him, he is implicitly trusted. Success appears full, but the truth goes deeper: "If you ask them who is brave—who is true—who is just—who is it they would trust with their lives?—they would say, Tuan Jim. And yet they can never know the real, real truth" (305). Jim wants to feel the "certitude of rehabilitation," but unresolved guilt prevents him from feeling completely worthy of the natives' heroic conception of him. "Upon my soul and conscience," he says to Marlow, "if such a thing can be forgotten, then I think I have a right to dismiss it from my mind" (305). But forgetting is impossible, and for Conrad good works do not constitute penance, as Jim's continuing uneasiness, self-mistrust, and need for reassurance attest. The defect of character remains. Conrad wants to believe in the redemptive possibilities of action even while he concedes grudgingly its inadequacy and acknowledges the inevitable necessity of punishment. With poignant irony, Jim becomes captive to the very things which make him lord. Enslavement to his dream has become externalized. The imagery of imprisonment used in describing Jim throughout the novel (31, 102, 247, 262, 283) prepares us for this closing-in of fate, darkening Jim with an aura of destiny. Once Jim believed he could begin again with a clean slate, but now he senses the imperishability of the past, the endurance of conscience, and the limitation of human desire.

Into Patusan's storybook reality steps Gentleman Brown, an Iago figure, a vehicle of fate and legate from the Western world. A convincing figure in his own right, he is also a grotesque parody of Jim. In their dramatic encounter, the two confront each other separated

by a muddy creek, "but standing on the opposite poles of that conception of life which includes all mankind" (381). However, absolute
divisions do not exist for Conrad, and, significantly, the creek is muddy.
Though Jim in his superiority would like to think he and Brown are
antithetical, just as he attempted to distance himself from the *Patna*
deserters, Conrad implies their similarity before he demonstrates it.
The anonymity of their names, a first and last name respectively,
suggests both men are to be seen as a single identity. Now leaders,
the two are outcasts and romantic wanderers whose pasts contained
a shattering experience which they took to heart. Brown is horrified
at actual imprisonment, Jim by the prison of his past, and both men
pursue the illusion of freedom through individual action. Each sees
himself victimized by fate, Jim in his claim that he was caught unawares, Brown in the death of the missionary's wife he abducted and
seemed to have loved. Each is intent on working out a private plan:
Brown seeks vengeance on the world to demonstrate his supremacy,
whereas Jim searches for a means to both realize and redeem himself. Each pursues a fixed idea, but Jim's worthy effort shares with
Brown's malevolence a fundamental hubris. An English decency and
the exigency to regain honor act to restrain and give moral direction
to Jim's egotism, but although Jim is no Kurtz and Patusan is not
the savage interior of the Congo, Brown forces the recognition of
the criminal potential inherent in Jim's position of extraordinary
power.

Brown senses immediately that this commanding figure is his natural adversary. Seizing upon Jim as a challenge, a prey, Brown proceeds diabolically to ferret out his enemy's weakness:

> And there ran through the rough talk a vein of subtle reference to
> their common blood, an assumption of common experience; a sick-
> ening suggestion of common guilt, of secret knowledge that was like
> a bond of their minds and of their hearts. (387)

Baines argues, wrongly I think, that Jim's actions were unaffected
by Brown's innuendos. By European standards Jim was honorable
in liberating Brown and not paralyzed mentally; he could not have
foreseen Brown's treachery.[12] But Jim is callow to the point that he
believes literally in words and personal pledges. Does Brown merit
such trust? Everyone else—admittedly all nonwhite—recognizes im-

mediately the extreme danger; trusting the invaders is unthinkable. Why Jim's susceptibility to accepting Brown's version of events, why the precipitate haste in letting Brown go, why no prolonged and careful examination of the situation? In the face of a crisis that demands absolute, cold clarity, Jim prevails upon Doramin and the populace not by argument but by invoking his person. Seemingly, he imputes to Brown something of his own chivalrous standards. But beneath that naiveté and failure to measure the man critically is Jim's inability to face Brown, to confess similarity, to stand up to Brown's words and tone of accusation. Realistically, Brown is the prisoner, yet Jim allows the trapped man to set the terms of release, to demand and retain his weapons. Jim's submission reveals the dire consequences of his identification with the other and his unresolved guilt. At the same time, Jim's freeing of Brown has striking parallels with his *Patna* desertion. Both instances are betrayals of public trust because of cowardice stemming from excessive individualism. In his assumption of superiority, Jim does not recognize obligations he does not feel, the claims of imposed or implicit duty. Fear during the *Patna* crisis was natural, but never having given strong allegiance to maritime values and discipline, Jim failed under stress to resist that fear in the performance of duty. In Patusan, his inability to resist the impulses Brown releases in him, his anxiety to shield himself, leads him to repeat a failure to execute the burden of leadership. Without explaining why, Jim refuses, in a further display of irresponsibility, personally to escort the whites out of Patusan. It is Jim who is in flight, shirking reminders of his own imperfection, trying to preserve an undefiled self-image. Morf asserts Jim's sympathy with Brown and states that identification is "characterized always by an extraordinary indulgence for the second self, an indulgence which of necessity remains incomprehensible to any other person. . . . Jim's indulgence for Brown is typical. He simply cannot resist the evil *because the evil is within himself.*"[13] Van Ghent comments that Jim judges Brown as he judged himself, "as a victim of circumstances . . . rather than as a character exposed by circumstances, at least to be given that benefit of doubt which would discriminate intention from deed."[14] However, in Conrad's moral terms, it must be added, the element of self-pity implicit in Jim's release of Brown marks the act as sentimental and cowardly. Brown is asking for another opportunity, a preciously personal request for Jim, who cannot withhold from another what he himself has so fervently sought and been granted. Later, when Jewel asks if the intruders are very bad, Jim's response has the accent of self-reflection: "Men act badly sometimes without being much worse than others" (394).[15]

On the meaning of Jim's conduct toward Brown, surprisingly Marlow is neither probing nor critical. Guerard points out the danger of trusting Marlow as a reliable guide to Conrad's convictions and final decisions and furthermore cautions against overvaluing Marlow's commentary. "Marlow has repeatedly taken us in. He is a considerably more lenient witness than his austere moralizing tone suggests. On various occasions he brings in the damaging evidence . . . very casually and digressively, as though inviting us to overlook it."[16] Marlow's observations on Jim's treatment of Brown, plausible as they are, nevertheless, tend to favor Jim. "It is evident that he did not mistrust Brown; there was no reason to doubt the story, whose truth seemed warranted by the rough frankness, by a sort of virile sincerity in accepting the morality and consequences of his act" (394). That the leader of a band of armed intruders, surrounded and fighting a losing battle, would not resort to guile is never considered as a possibility. By having Marlow side with Jim in this instance, Conrad deflects attention from what is morally blameworthy in Jim's decision. Another example of narrator sympathy at a crucial moment which obscures the deeper nature of the hero's irresponsibility occurs in *Under Western Eyes,* where the language teacher's presentation of Razumov's surrender of Haldin to the police seems to imply a tacit sanction. If Jim appears honorable in freeing Brown, yet another victim of the savage brigand, one may be less apt to scrutinize Jim's motives and bearing in accepting the death penalty. At one point, Marlow goes so far as to affirm that Jim had achieved "greatness," a summing-up that may comfort Marlow but which seems inadequate morally.

Jim's indulgence and Brown's murderousness are in large part reactions to what each perceives symbolically in the other. Brown detests Jim's handsome youth, standoffish air, and impeccable dress, "from the white helmet to the canvas leggings and the pipe-clayed shoes, which in Brown's sombre irritated eyes seemed to belong to things he had in the very shaping of his life contemned and flouted"

(380).[17] Jim seems to represent the decent world from which Brown has excluded himself, and perhaps he glimpses in Jim his own lost possibilities, what he might have been or was. Such a reminder must be destroyed. Brown attempts to insinuate their equality, to soil this man of lofty bearing, to give the lie to Jim's illusion of faultlessness. And, above all, Jim cannot stand to be dirtied. I do not, as Van Ghent does, understand Jim's freeing of Brown as being a lonely act of faith with the white men "out there."[18] If Jim's pledge with Brown is his way of keeping faith, he certainly takes no pride in it. His lingering sadness about "out there" adds poignance to his exile, but he does not rationalize his deed as a gesture of fidelity to his heritage. When Jim persuades Doramin and the chieftains to release the band fully armed, he declares, "Everyone shall be safe." He, too, is included in that reckless guarantee.

Given the opportunity, Brown exploits Cornelius's scheme and vents his misanthropy by attacking Dain Waris's party. But "even in this awful outbreak there is a superiority as of a man who carries right— the abstract thing—within the envelope of his common desires. It was not a vulgar and treacherous massacre; it was a lesson, a retribution" (404). Brown acts out his personal vision, what Marlow, after a deathbed interview with him, phrases as the "illusion of having trampled all the earth under his feet" (384). Dying wretchedly, Brown, nevertheless, revels in a perverse glory in having paid off "the stuck-up beggar after all," gleams with a defiant, malicious satisfaction inspired by righteousness and achievement (344). Despite the grotesqueness of the comparison, Brown expires believing he is fulfilled in purpose as does Jim. The self-enclosure and consuming devotion to a fixed idea manifest in Brown's demise comment implicitly on the meaning and moral dimensions of Jim's death.

Lord Jim is not the proper material nor Jim the substantial figure necessary for a mature expression of Conrad's conception of integrity, a conception which flows from his tragic vision. An unsatisfactory resolution of the theme of guilt and expiation, the novel's conclusion is also a retreat, a holding back from the truths discovered in "Heart of Darkness." Conrad wants to salvage some redeeming and affirmative belief through Jim even while he criticizes the romantic claims his death seems to promote. Here, Conrad's complicated attitude toward his character expresses itself as protectiveness without moral assent. Conrad knows that consciousness and what would follow—acknowledged guilt, loss of ideal self-image—would break Jim, make impossible the resolve and composure with which he meets execution. Conrad will go further in his treatment of the romantic in *Nostromo,* where he dramatizes Nostromo's dissolution of identity precipitated by failure, consciousness, and guilt brought on by betrayal. The proud silence with which Jim takes the bullet, while consistent psychologically, seems also to reflect Conrad's necessity to administer punishment in terms that will dignify Jim but which Conrad cannot fully respect. One sign of Conrad's reservations is his with-holding of sympathy; Jim's death is unmoving. By contrast, in the later novels Emilia succors a dying Nostromo and Tekla embraces Razumov without qualification in his agony of greatest need. In its pitilessness, Jim's death resembles Leggatt's retributive exile. Con-rad's moral austerity is seldom tempered by an earned and unsen-timental compassion.

When Tamb' tells Jim of the disaster and how it is unsafe for his man to go out amongst the people, Marlow reports Jim's dawning recognition: "Then Jim understood. He had retreated from one world, for a small matter of an impulsive jump, and now the other, the work of his own hands, had fallen in ruins upon his head" (408). Knowing Jim could not survive the terrible effects of introspection, yet moved, nevertheless, to keep him within heroic dimensions, Conrad must gloss over Jim's period of moral reflection. What little he compre-hends is told, not dramatized, not worked out painfully in conscious-ness. The cost of this strategy is a shallow rendering of Jim's guilt and remorse. Though no formal code is operative, Jim has estab-lished the terms of his own commitment; in pledging his life as guar-antee for everyone's safety, he has become trapped by his own ego-tism. Jim seems to render his own verdict and to effect his own punishment. But if taking death upon himself is payment for the consequences of setting Brown free, it reflects also Jim's adherence to the imperatives of his romantic heroism, a final opportunity for extraordinary behavior. Unresolved guilt continued to plague him after the *Patna* trial because he could not reconcile his dereliction with his self-image. Guilt and retribution are dealt with now in ro-mantic terms, which is to say that Jim's claims of egotism are ad-vanced even as his embrace of punishment signifies self-repudiation. "The central ambiguities and the two sides of honor—guilt or disgrace? act of ritual atonement or act of pride?—follow him to the last moments of his life."[19] However, what is implicit in Jim's decision to die is that he senses the collapse of vital illusions—of being able to transcend the past and win a future through self-affirming action, of having atoned for one disreputable act by honorable success and an exemplary life. With no place else to go, nothing further to fight for, Jim says to Tamb', "I have no life." His fatal destiny has at last blocked all avenues of flight. Just as he had appeared deliberately at the *Patna* trial, he marches to accept death from the stricken father.

Jim is "false" in Jewel's eyes because he deserts her after having sworn loyalty. In the novel, however, her condemnation, though necessary and just, is not given the emphasis and force to diminish Jim. Moreover, in Conrad's best art love never fares well, human relationships do not flourish, and the demands of individualism take precedence over fidelity to the beloved. The more telling criticism, more in keeping with Conrad's own values, is not that Jim betrays a loving woman but that his moral awareness and hence anguish never go deeper than the surface, never get past his egotism. "Nothing can touch me," he responds to Jewel's charge that he will not defend himself. Indeed, it is because very little can penetrate Jim's consciousness that Conrad withholds his respect. In counterpoint to Jewel's accusation of falsity is Stein's insistence that Jim is "true," faithful to his dream. But Stein's advocacy of the idealism of self brings no consolation. The old man's gesture of waving farewell to his butterflies closes the novel on a note of fatigued resignation as he awaits approaching death. The bleak, unsparing conclusion to "Heart of Darkness" is here softened to a mood of darkening melancholy at the sadness of things.

Evaluating Marlow's assertion that Jim was "great" is more complicated. Jim is a type, and he has realized the possibilities of his nature individualistically. In him, Conrad has carried the idea of his romantic hero to its apogee. Jim must die in the flush of youth because he could never mature in the author's rigorous terms, which go beyond Marlow's tentative reservations. Jim's final act may seem to convey higher values, but Conrad's art presents implicit and serious criticism. The quality of self-glorification in Jim's willed punishment before an awestruck populace inheres in the very nature of his romantic egotism and is one of its weaknesses. True, civil conflict is averted though Conrad does not underscore this point and Jim scarcely considers it. Although he pays the extreme debt to the community, Jim also avoids having to struggle with a future devoid of romantic possibilities. Clearly, the moral significance of his death is no simple expression of self-sacrifice for the communal good or act of self-repudiation compelled by remorse. The suggestion of defiance as Jim stares unflinchingly at his executioner resembles to some degree Brown's triumph in his death throes; how far Jim has emerged from self-centeredness remains problematical. Hatless when he jumped from the *Patna*, Jim is also bareheaded when he faces Doramin, a detail suggestive of moral deficiency, perhaps a want of full manhood.[20] Shot through the chest, Jim falls forward "with his hand over his lips," a gesture seemingly meant to stifle a cry but recalling more importantly Jim's lack of verbal defense or explanation at the official inquiry.[21] Even if Jim's silent act is supposed to speak for him, the equivocalness of that act, its multifarious and conflicting meanings, calls attention to an unsettled problem in Conrad's fiction. In the face of betrayal and disillusionment, Conrad has not yet formulated an affirmation in which he can believe. Undeniably, Conrad's universe forces a response in the reader of anxiety and uncertainty, encourages an attitude of doubt regarding all values, but here, I would suggest, the working out of Jim's fate reflects more an artistic limitation than a statement of ambiguity as a novelistic and philosophical idea.

Though expressed tentatively, growth of consciousness and the moral voice emerged as significant values in "Heart of Darkness." One reason Marlow asserted Kurtz's greatness was that he had something to say at the "last opportunity for pronouncement" before madness and death claimed him. To speak with conviction at the extreme moment is of preeminent importance for Conrad and suggests an exigent and continuing struggle for conscience, all the more arduous because of the depths of his nihilism. Jim dies without a voice of his own, expiring at his peak though "untouched," suffering minimized by one shot and near-instantaneous death. Frozen into ideal image and form, unmarred in death, proud to the last, Jim moves into story, legend, myth, but he does not achieve the stature of a Conradian tragic hero. Only Razumov will prove equal to Conrad's severest test, gain his unequivocal assent, and earn his rare compassion.

CHAPTER FOUR

Nostromo: Versions of Failure

I

EARNEST, capable, high-minded, Charles Gould embodies the nine-teenth-century spirit of individualism, conquest, and industry. Grounded in the English decencies, ambitious but not self-aggran-dizing, Gould is a serious and impressive representative of capital-ism. The equestrian statue of Charles IV to which he is linked adds associations of regal nobility, power, and martial ardor. Gould's as-pirations are infused with a sense of mission both personal and ideo-logical. With determination made more powerful by a sense of filial obligation bent on redeeming his father's wasted life and with the conviction that the mine will be the vehicle of a just social order, Gould dedicates himself to an enterprise heroic in the difficulties to be overcome and apparently virtuous in aim. Where the father was despairing and inept, worn out by the land, the son brings youth and outlook freshened in England, a self-assurance unconditioned by tragic experience, a belief in remedy through work done in the right way. Plausible in its pragmatic idealism, nevertheless, Gould's blind faith in the benefits of the mine is the flawed rationale of cap-italism:

> Only let the material interests once get a firm footing, and they are bound to impose the conditions on which alone they can continue to

exist. That's how your moneymaking is justified here in the face of lawlessness and disorder. It is justified because the security which it demands must be shared with an oppressed people. A better justice will come afterwards. That's your ray of hope.[1]

One detects here an echo of Marlow's belief in efficiency as the re-deeming hope of imperialist conquest. If efficiency is wholly absent in the Congo of "Heart of Darkness," its realization in Costaguana carries unforeseen perils: efficiency's voracious and autonomous ap-petite, diminution of human values, and growing and organized class opposition. Since Gould identifies utterly with the mine, an identi-fication which of necessity becomes obsessive and desperate, Gould's failure can be read as an indictment of capitalism itself. Despite his motives, regardless of the admirable personal effort and risk, the effect of his work is the same as if executed by an unscrupulous em-pire-builder.

The railroad engineer, noteworthy for his competence, courage, and impartiality, remarks that "things seem to be worth nothing by what they are in themselves. I begin to believe that the only solid thing about them is the spiritual value which everyone discovers in his own form of activity" (318). As an expression of Conrad's con-tinuing concern with the problem of belief, it is worth noting the novel's many figures who give allegiance to something higher: Avellanos's classical liberalism, Antonia's patriotism, Father Cor-belàn's religious politics, Viola's heroic republicanism, Emilia's faith in humane values, Decoud's love for Antonia, Monygham's chival-rous loyalty to Mrs. Gould, Don Pépé's soldierly fidelity to Charles, Holroyd's purer form of Christianity. Even Mitchell, wed to the ship-ping company, relates his efforts to progress and historic moment. On its public side, the vindication and spiritual value of the mine reside for Gould in the law, good faith, order, and security he is certain will result. However, Gould infuses a material pursuit with a transcendence it cannot support. Cherishing idealized action, Conrad is at the same time sharply critical of the extremes of such ideali-zation: failures in moral perception, inflexibility, ruthlessness. Ob-serving Father Corbelàn, whose politics are motivated by a reaction-ary zeal to restore confiscated church properties, Decoud notes the extreme wrongheadedness into which an honest, almost sacred, con-viction may drive a man. "'It is like madness. It must be—because it's self-destructive.' It seemed to him that every conviction, as soon as it became effective, turned into that form of dementia the gods send upon those they wish to destroy" (200). In Charles Gould this theme of belief as demon receives its fullest elaboration.

In his supreme confidence that the mining venture will bring all he envisages, Gould is a romantic, the self-deceived idealist who appears so often in Conrad's pages. Despite his sober practicality, he holds exaggerated claims for his project, never questions whether his hoped-for order is possible or desirable, never weighs the costs it may exact on his personal life or on the life of the people. Gould cannot afford the hazards of reflection. Decoud is incisive in his disdain of Charles's sentimentalism, a characteristic meant to be associated with the England that educated him, which means simply that Gould "cannot act or exist without idealizing every simple feeling, desire, or achievement. He could not believe his own motives if he did not make them first a part of some fairy tale. The earth is not quite good enough for him" (214–15). If idealizing one's motives leads to falsification and misjudgment, Decoud's despiritualizing attitude and his "erecting passions into duties" reduce commitment to the purely subjective, carry the risk of nihilism when passion loses its force or object. Gould's fixed idea of justice becomes an extension and expression of his egotism so that to idealize the mine has the effect of self-idealization, blocking self-scrutiny.

Only success could justify the compromises Gould makes with his conscience, acquiescing in bribery for the sake of peace. Costaguana's lawlessness makes any immediate alternative to this practice unfeasible, but what is revealed in addition are deficiencies Gould shares with capitalism, a narrowness of vision and an amorality in the pursuit of ends. Business dictates a need for absolute political disinterest, seen in Gould's stern but courteous professional aloofness (a reticence extended also to his wife, private self being absorbed by public role), in a refusal to protest unsavory payoffs. Gould's deepest wish is to be left alone so he can get on with his work, precisely the student Razumov's attitude in *Under Western Eyes,* an unwise expectation in a society without democratic roots and an impulse toward isolation that the world denies all Conrad's significant men. This initial tolerance of prevailing conditions links Gould with Monygham's conservatism, though with the important difference that Gould believes

social betterment will evolve out of work. Charles practices a strin-
gent self-discipline as both expedient policy and moral defense, but
this posture proves unavailing. His concession to the country's unprincipled elements erodes his self-esteem, a moral wound which will
deepen as the mine, despite its legitimacy under Ribiera, slowly brings
its own form of injustice.

The novel's controlling attitude toward politics is profoundly pessimistic, conservative to the point of favoring non-involvement regardless of conditions, even while acknowledging that such disengagement cannot be maintained. When Gould ends his neutrality by
backing Ribiera, whose reformist program, Gould thinks, besides its
higher considerations, will better serve his mine, the omniscient narrator regards this decision as a serious lapse. "The mine had corrupted his judgment by making him sick of bribing and intriguing
merely to have his work left alone from day to day" (364–65). Decoud
mistrusts Gould's view of things, including of course his politics, and
Monygham disapproves strongly of Gould's partisanship (specifically, ordering the silver shipment out of Sulaco), averring that Montero can be bought in the usual way. To join Ribiera is to espouse
insurrection, and the novel disavows political violence, regardless of
its cause or aim, and it sees reform as ineffectual. With Ribiera's success, Gould has gained a dubious victory at a large price, a victory
that carries the seeds of instability and new injustice. Conrad shows
politics as illusory and corrupting, a dangerous form of romanticism,
out of whose widespread debris emerge only individual acts of heroism.

Although limited in apprehension, Gould does suffer jarring glints
of recognition. Because of cultural conditioning and insufficient modes
of perception fashioned on assumptions of rationality, measure, and
progress, the Westerners are unable to comprehend the alien and
primitive forces of Costaguana. Gould, however, grasps a frightening
insight in conversation with Monygham: "The words one knows so
well have a nightmarish meaning in this country. Liberty, democracy,
patriotism, government—all of them have a flavour of folly and
murder" (408). When necessity coerces him into uneasy alliance with
the notorious Hernandez, Gould is struck by the parting words of
the brigand's emissary, who asks if the master of the mine has any
message to send to the master of the Campo:

> The truth of the comparison struck Charles Gould heavily. In his de-
> termined purpose he held the mine, and the indomitable bandit held
> the Campo by the same precarious tenure. They were equals before
> the lawlessness of the land. It was impossible to disentangle one's ac-
> tivity from its debasing contacts. A close-meshed net of crime and cor-
> ruption lay upon the whole country. An immense and weary discour-
> agement sealed his lips for a time. (401)

This sudden identification with outlawry diminishes Gould's over-
prized sense of right, forces him to see that he, too, shares in the
country's moral contagion. This familiar Conradian confrontation of
apparent moral opposites—the mine owner realizes for him there
are no external checks—precedes and affords a perspective on Gould's
extreme assumption of his power.

When Gould threatens the victorious Montero with exploding the
mine, playing his last argument to save his life and the mine's autonomy, it is misleading to say that Gould has violated his abstract
values because of unrestrained egoism, perverting the moral order
by subordinating his ideals to the mine.[2] To put the matter thus is
to imply a judgment of immorality that is not borne out by the text.
A failure in restraint signals invariably a descent into evil for Conrad,
but here the case is more complicated. For one thing, Gould's tactic
is effective; it does intimidate Montero into releasing him. Afterward, Gould confesses to Monygham that if not for his threat, he
would not have been freed. Furthermore, to surrender the mine would
entail Gould's order absolving Pépé and his men from its defense,
and it is Pépé's initiative in attacking Sulaco later which saves Gould
from execution and contributes to a Ribierist victory. Rather, what
stands revealed emphatically by Gould's willingness to use dynamite
is the life and death bond between the man and his possession. "This
resolution expressed the tenacity of his character, the remorse of that
subtle conjugal infidelity through which his wife was no longer the
sole mistress of his thoughts, something of his father's imaginative
weakness, and something, too, of the spirit of a buccaneer throwing
a lighted match into the magazine rather than surrender his ship"
(365–56). Abstract principles for Conrad are always suspect, usually
crumbling before the onslaught of experience. What alternative is
there? A patriotic principle might see the mine as belonging to the
country, its raison d'être, regardless of directorship, to serve Costa-

guana. Of course, without Gould the operation would flounder, certainly for many years, and financial backing would collapse in the wake of Holroyd's defection. For Gould to serve Montero is both intolerable and perilous, and expropriation would ruin the mine's viability. The melodramatic denouement to the Sulaco fighting, the fortuitousness of Barrios's and Pépé's near-simultaneous arrival and Gould's last second rescue (Monygham is also just saved, the hangman's rope on his neck), seems to remove Gould's threat of violence from a settled moral category and place his action in a military context. Gould is in a position of unofficial military command by virtue of his armed workers and his support of Ribiera. Though Gould acts to control his mine, that end serves Ribiera. Amidst civil war and the politics of revolution, desperate measures become unavoidable. More, they are demanded. The lawlessness of the land and the overwhelming sweep of events claim the "King of Sulaco" as they did Hernandez; respectability and criminality become determined primarily by history. Hernandez is praised as a hero and elevated to minister of war under the victorious regime. Gould's threat, then, must be seen as amoral.

Revolutionary upheaval exposes dramatically the inimical underside of Gould's passion, but the contingency of blowing up the mine had been fixed upon earlier. The fatality inherent in his attachment to the mine grows out of the bone of his character. "If ever a man has fetichized the production of commodities, if ever a man has surrendered his self to his social role, it is Charles Gould. The sterility of the mine is the sterility of his marriage, the public failure both cause and magnified reflection of his private failure."[3] In the end, Gould has not learned; his ruinous egotism, though bruised, remains essentially unchanged, his destiny is sealed. He cannot lessen his addiction to the mine, which would entail an acceptance of limitation, a need for moral revision, an admission of defeat. The unredeemed self-destructiveness of Gould's fate, an indication of Conrad's implicit moral judgment, is evident in his willful refusal to see critically, in his continued neglect of Emilia, in the drying up of his sources of belief and feeling, and in the futile self-sacrifice of his work. *Nostromo* offers no ray of hope for either Gould or Costaguana. In the tortured vision of Mrs. Gould, alone in all her sadness, a final despairing image looms:

She saw the San Tomé mountain hanging over the Campo, over the whole land, feared, hated, wealthy; more soulless than any tyrant, more pitiless and autocratic than the worst Government; ready to crush innumerable lives in the expansion of its greatness. He did not see it. He could not see it. It was not his fault. He was perfect. . . . she saw clearly the San Tomé mine possessing, consuming, burning up the life of the last of the Costaguana Goulds; mastering the energetic spirit of the son as it had mastered the lamentable weakness of the father. (521–22)

II

EMILIA is the perfect complement to Charles, the wife he needs so that he can embrace his mission. Responding to Charles's "competency," which she senses will give her definition and form, Emilia is struck "from the first by his unsentimentalism, by that very quietude of mind which she had erected in her thought for a sign of perfect competency in the business of living" (50). Cloistered and inexperienced, she has no way of knowing that his mastery does not extend to the realm of intimacy. Marriage to Charles carries the appeal of a high purpose, offers the glamor of an exotic land and the challenge of forging a new existence and a massive enterprise in difficult circumstances. "All the eagerness of youth for a strange life, for great distances, for a future in which there was an air of adventure, of combat—a subtle thought of redress and conquest, had filled her with an intense excitement" (65). Though Conrad imagines her in traditional terms, as a wife whose essence is devotion and communal effort, he gives to the shape of her career his vital pattern of youthful romanticization ending in disillusionment and terrible knowledge.

What sets her apart fundamentally from the distinctive Conradian protagonists is her selflessness and self-sacrifice. Lacking the independence and egotism of Conrad's usual male heroes, she is not the character to dramatize effectively those themes crucial to Conrad's conception of integrity: striving for an ego-ideal, the conflict between conscience and impulse, the problem of belief. Emilia's weakly realized betrayal motif (yielding to Decoud's persuasion that the silver shipment must proceed, even she withholds from Charles news of a Ribierist military defeat), though unconvincing as an instance of

Emilia's wrongdoing and unessential to the plot, does indicate the importance in which Conrad holds her despite the limitation of the woman's role he faced with her character. Conrad does not raise the issue of Emilia's complicity in Charles's failure. Having embraced his aims, she comes to see their ruinousness, but perhaps because she is a woman and a wife, she does not take full responsibility for her part, however subordinate, in that failure. Betrayal and guilt are treated substantially in Monygham, related to Emilia by principles of self-denial and service. While she comes understandably to share Charles's moral conception of the mine and to take an idealized view of success, her belief lacks his fierceness, abstractness, and totality. She never loses her human quality. In a delicate touch, both ironic and moving, Conrad gives her awed response to the initial bar of silver maternal overtones. "She had laid her unmercenary hands, with an eagerness that made them tremble, upon the first silver ingot turned out still warm from the mould; and by her imaginative estimate of its power she endowed that lump of metal with a justificative conception, as though it were not a mere fact, but something far-reaching and impalpable, like the true expression of an emotion or the emergence of a principle" (107). Their marriage, one recalls, is childless. In the one area where she might have a more direct influence, in critical discussions with her husband, she bows to his reticence, which more than anything sets the tone of their relationship, to his competence, to his argument of native birth. Emilia is unprobing by nature, and as a foreigner, she is not in a position to raise questions of pith and challenge. Moreover, he is not a man to be dissuaded, and he has his own reasons for refusing to discuss "the ethical view" of his policies.

Except for their brief courtship, the love scenes and moments of intimacy are minimal, and while this absence registers the increasing sterility of the marriage, it also spares Conrad the difficulty he has in dramatizing sexually charged episodes. One consequence is that Emilia, though never stiff or lifeless, seems more than ever an idealized figure, Madonna-like. By the end of the novel, however, the conception of her as a secular saint becomes poignantly ironic. With the blighting of her sources of inspiration and support, her deeper emotions imprisoned, reduced to social function, she seems miniaturized and frozen amid the splendid interior of her old Spanish house, universally revered but unloved as a wife. Emilia comes to mourn her husband as her guardian aunt the Marchesa, "nun-like in her black robes and a white band over the forehead," grieved for the marquis, who died for his country. And the poverty of the Marchesa's widowhood, which had "the austerity of a sacrifice offered to a noble ideal," is reproduced in the emotional deprivation of Emilia's marriage, sacrificed also for an ideal, so that neither Emilia nor Charles escapes the grim shadow of family heritage.

To the critics' widespread admiration of Mrs. Gould, Irving Howe adds a qualifying note:

> Mrs. Gould is all kindness, all goodness, all charity; entirely alert to the most "delicate shades of self-forgetfulness"; but she does not live in Costaguana, she has sealed herself off in an enclave of disciplined suffering. The court she holds for the Europeans and a few chosen "natives" is merely a mirror to her loneliness; the life of the country on which her comfort depends remains a secret forever closed to her. . . . The rhythms of Costaguana are alien to her racial conventions, and because she cannot transcend those conventions—because she lacks the boldness of Mrs. Moore in *Passage to India*—her life narrows into a ritual of controlled deprivation. Lovely and luminous as she seems in her devotion to personal values, Mrs. Gould signifies the incompleteness of trying to live merely by those values.[4]

Although in Conrad's terms suffering is not a mark of disapproval, Emilia's plight does convey a sense of hopelessness and waste. What is missing with the collapse of her realm of private feeling is the possibility of wholehearted service to the country. For Conrad, however, exile closes off this avenue of purpose and redemption. Nevertheless, what distinguishes Mrs. Gould in the end are solitary anguish, resignation without loss of compassion, continued dedication to the community in her limited capacity as a foreigner, and, importantly, tragic knowledge—grasped unflinchingly—moral qualities which carry Conrad's unequivocal respect. Given the extent of her loss and the realities of Costaguana society, it seems improbable that she could find alternative values by entering the life of the country, even if such an idea had occurred to her. Indeed, it is only with Natalie of *Under Western Eyes* that Conrad will create a woman who, despite the withering of love, will be able to go forward confidently in a life now wed to deprivation and hardship. Significantly, Natalie returns home to Russia to devote herself to patriotic endeavor.

Isolation from her husband, disillusionment, and a sense of defeat and futility bring Emilia a clear-sighted perception of the desolation that is her life:

> It had come into her mind that for life to be large and full, it must contain the care of the past and of the future in every passing moment of the present. Our daily work must be done to the glory of the dead, and for the good of those who come after. She thought that, and sighed without opening her eyes—without moving at all. Mrs. Gould's face became set and rigid for a second, as if to receive, without flinching, a great wave of loneliness that swept over her head. And it came into her mind, too, that no one would ever ask her with solicitude what she was thinking of. No one. No one . . . who could be answered with careless sincerity in the ideal perfection of confidence. (520–21)

In the depth of her suffering and in her grasp of the darkest realities, Mrs. Gould endures the fullest burden of tragedy in the novel. She is sorrowfully aware of all that has been lost—her chance for happiness in love, Charles's possibilities for fulfillment, the radiant dream of redemption. Without evasion, self-pity, or sentimentality, she confronts a vision of the future as despairing as it is undeniable:

> Incorrigible in his devotion to the great silver mine was the Señor Administrador! Incorrigible in his hard, determined service of the material interests to which he had pinned his faith in the triumph of order and justice. Poor boy! She had a clear vision of the grey hairs on his temples. He was perfect—perfect. What more could she have expected? It was a colossal and lasting success; and love was only a short moment of forgetfulness, a short intoxication, whose delight one remembered with a sense of sadness. . . . There was something inherent in the necessities of successful action which carried with it the moral degradation of the idea. She saw the San Tomé mountain hanging over the Campo, over the whole land, feared, hated, wealthy; more soulless than any tyrant, more pitiless and autocratic than the worst Government; ready to crush innumerable lives in the expansion of its greatness. He did not see it. He could not see it. It was not his fault. He was perfect, perfect; but she would never have him to herself. . . . she saw clearly the San Tomé mine possessing, consuming, burning up the life of the last of the Costaguana Goulds; mastering the energetic spirit of the son as it had mastered the lamentable weakness of the father. A terrible success. . . . With a prophetic vision she saw herself surviving alone the degradation of her young ideal of life, of love, of work—all alone in the Treasure House of the World. The

profound, blind, suffering expression of a painful dream settled on
her face with its closed eyes. In the indistinct voice of an unlucky sleeper,
lying passive in the grip of a merciless nightmare, she stammered out
aimlessly the words—
"Material interest." (521–22)

Emilia's charitable lie, a rebuke to Monygham's urge to expose, at-
tests to her unimpaired humanity and confirms her repudiation of
the material interests, an independent act which separates her morally from her husband.

III

DECOUD and Monygham come naturally into comparison as aspects
of Conrad's radical skepticism which breeds detachment. Decoud is
skepticism tempered by social instincts; Monygham's skepticism has
hardened to misanthropy. Absent from Decoud's disbelief is Monygham's depth of bitterness and acerbity of temper. Certainly, Decoud
is satiric and pointed, but there is often to his intelligence an element
of brilliant display, of restless energy seeking exercise and audience.
He has not yet frozen into a life attitude, whereas Monygham speaks
often with an accent of finality. The 50-year-old doctor's nihilism
and mordancy are rooted in his own tragic history; the younger man's
skepticism, proceeding from a sense of intellectual superiority and
cosmopolitan pretension, is not grounded in self-knowledge and critical experience. Exile and the inferior status of one's homeland, though
they necessarily affect a man's bearing in the world, are insufficient
in themselves to account for either Decoud's dilettantism or his skepticism. This element of callowness links Decoud with many of Conrad's vulnerable heroes. That Decoud's attitude is untested and essentially unearned is crucial, for to sustain skepticism under duress
demands a toughness and resilience he lacks, and he is fatally unaware of the corrosive power of mind, particularly when turned inward. Deep personal adversity, the significant distinction between the
pair, has rid Monygham of egotism and connection to society. The
untried Decoud, though, is more dependent on society than he knows,
overvalues himself (intellect being the source and expression of his
egotism), and tends to be uncommitted out of disdain for the irra-

tional and farcical he sees in life. About action, however, Decoud is
ambivalent, willing to be seduced to an enterprise his mind may mock
or consider futile. His sense of disengagement is less pronounced
than Monygham's resignation. Neither has the moral belief that sus-
tains or which impels a man to strenuous action, and it takes a woman
to call forth their best instincts, though Decoud responds also to his
unvoiced patriotism.

Decoud is discerning and lucid, and both his pessimism and scorn
are amply justified in the novel. Decoud's response to his worldview
is to keep his distance from experience, and authorial criticism centers on Decoud's lack of moral seriousness, the seriousness that can
only come from struggle with life. For an austere moralist like Conrad, the charge of wastefulness and superficiality carries considerable
sting. More substantially, however, the implication of Decoud's attitude of obeying only passion and intelligence (an attitude at variance
with his deeper impulses) is a dangerous individualism, recognizing
no authority beyond the self. Though an Iago might just as easily
espouse such a position, the peril for Decoud lies not in criminal
excess but in a vulnerability to an extreme situation where passion
and intelligence are wholly inadequate. In Decoud, Conrad plays out
the consequences of an undeveloped conscience in a civilized man.
One point implied by the novel and by Decoud's case in particular
is that for belief to be won, it must be earned at "home," that is, in
the politics of patriotism and revolution. The energizing illusions that
Conrad associated with romanticism (heroic adventure, individualism, geographical freedom) could not be sustained in his fiction. Belief for Conrad can only emerge at this stage in his career in a world
where this romanticism is impossible, though *Nostromo* is not that book.
This novel, however, points toward the concerns of *Under Western
Eyes,* a more comprehensive immersion in autobiographical material
than "Heart of Darkness" and one with obviously deeper personal
roots, closest and most dangerously "home" for Conrad. Outside his
homeland, Conrad suggests, Decoud must remain a poseur, cut off
from his emotional core, drifting into a kind of impostorship.

> He imagined himself Parisian to the tips of his fingers. But far from
> being that he was in danger of remaining a sort of nondescript dilet-
> tante all his life. He had pushed the habit of universal raillery to a

point where it blinded him to the genuine impulses of his own nature.
(153)

To aspire to be a European sophisticate and wit evokes admiration
from no one in the novel. His continental journalism is social play,
not professional effort. Paris may be glittering and stimulating, but
it offers him no opportunity of moral consequence, no significant
challenge.

That opportunity begins to shape itself in his godfather Don José's
summons of patriotic appeal, composed in Antonia's hand, entrust-
ing him with the clandestine purchase of European rifles for the
Ribierist cause. Stirred despite his own condescending attitude, Decoud accompanies the shipment to Costaguana, intending ostensibly
only a brief visit. Throwing up a comfortable, unadventurous existence at the thirty-year mark of one's life to go on a voyage of some
risk for deeper reasons than one can say bears a similarity to Marlow's situation in embarking for the Congo. One glimpses also in this
Decoud material Conrad's Marseilles experience and gunrunning
enterprise. But hailed as a patriot by the revered statesman, wel-
comed approvingly by Antonia, Decoud is drawn to submit to others'
expectations of him. Believing in nothing, he is gripped forcibly by
the community's sense of purpose and by the charged ambience. From
the distance of Europe he can refer to Costaguana politics as ludi-
crous, but once on its soil he feels the "absolute change of atmosphere. . . . He was moved in spite of himself by that note of passion and sorrow unknown on the more refined stage of European
politics" (156). Accepting the position of journalist, becoming increasingly involved in the lifeblood of his country, he is moved to admit
to himself, "I suppose I am more of a Costaguanero than I would
have believed possible" (176). His disavowal of the name of patriot
reflects both his scorn for that much abused designation and his independence ("the narrowness of every belief is odious"). Individualism, whether to woo Antonia or pursue his Separation plan, inter-
mingles with all Decoud's political activities. Though he acts like a
patriot and is sensitive, even passionate at times, about his country,
it is clear he does not have the completeness of belief of Don José,
Antonia, or Father Corbelàn. But while Conrad honors the claims of
patriotism, he is mistrustful because such devotion can lead readily

to fanaticism, self-deceit, ineptitude, the advancement of narrow interests. Does patriotism mean unquestioning fidelity under all circumstances, to be well spoken of by one's countrymen regardless of the quality of one's political intelligence? These issues become most acute when life and national integrity are at stake.

Half-way through the novel is the adventure in the Golfo Placido, the test of total darkness, a familiar and recurrent Conradian episode. The key position of this experience structurally and its dramatic intensity emphasize its significance: it marks the turning point in the destinies of two major figures. The presence on the craft of Hirsch, the dispossessed Jew, reminds us that Nostromo and Decoud are also outsiders in this non-European land. That Conrad makes Nostromo and Decoud shipmates calls attention to their similarity. Both men are utterly dependent on society; the Italian needs public acclaim and Decoud must have social activity, objects for his skepticism, and civilized safeguards from adversity and isolation. To a crucial extent, the community provides them with a definition of self. Each is now confronted with the unprecedented. When the Capataz extinguishes the boat's only candle (cf. the falling *Patna* masthead light in *Lord Jim* and the captain's lighted cigar which drops overboard when he spies Leggatt in "The Secret Sharer"), Decoud senses the dismaying uniqueness of his position:

> It was to Decoud as if his companion had destroyed, by a single touch, the world of affairs, of loves, of revolution, where his complacent superiority analyzed fearlessly all motives and all passions, including his own. . . . Intellectually self-confident, he suffered from being deprived of the only weapon he could use with effect. No intelligence could penetrate the darkness of the Placid Gulf. (275)

The isolation in this scene anticipates the terrible solitude that each will face afterward—and isolation is their supreme enemy. Hirsch represents, in an unobtrusive way, the hollowness of self and the treacherous internal forces that will destroy both protagonists. Undeniably, the hide merchant is dangerous cargo; symbolically, he is Nostromo's nemesis, incarnating his fear of failure and public ignominy, the specter of a pariah. Decoud's compassion—and need—for the terror-stricken man prevents Nostromo from killing him, and in so doing the stark moral difference between the two is illuminated. The manner of Hirsch's capture—being plucked out of the blackness by the transport's anchor—recalls other symbolic episodes in Conrad suggesting the irruption of the irrational, e.g., the submerged derelict striking the *Patna* and Leggatt emerging from the depths. Though Hirsch becomes a grotesquely ironic agent of betrayal, isolation brings out the corruptive elements of character that work to destroy Nostromo and Decoud.

Guerard's doubts about Decoud's suicide lead him to argue that Decoud's characterization "belongs with those in which a writer attempts to separate out and demolish a facet of himself by proxy. . . . Conrad may be condemning Decoud for a withdrawal and skepticism more radical than Decoud ever shows; which are, in fact, Conrad's own."[5] Howe remarks that in Decoud Conrad "violently tore at one of his major attitudes."[6] It is true that Conrad's withdrawal and skepticism are more radical than Decoud's, so radical, in fact, that he has not yet been able to sustain a convincing counterpoise, to formulate a belief to which he can commit himself. But it is not punishment or repudiation of Decoud's attitude that Conrad is dramatizing; rather, Conrad is testing Decoud's quality of resistance, the very heart of his moral substance, at the same time that he, Conrad, is seeking within himself resources of self-affirmation. The severity and intensely vivid evocation of Decoud's trial, the enormous pressure Conrad brings to bear on his exposed man indicate a vehemence suggestive of personal combat. Unquestionably, Conrad fears the implications of his own skepticism, particularly its costs when directed within and when concentrated on the most cherished elements of his romanticism. But for Conrad skepticism is also the vehicle to truth and integral to his imaginative vitality. Conrad's best art derives from the tensions aroused by his skepticism, and to condemn this aspect of himself would seem to be a form of artistic suicide. Conrad does partially condemn skepticism when he halts Monygham's attempt to root out Nostromo's crime, though as much to protect Nostromo as to censure Monygham. Furthermore, because Monygham's intellectual force in the novel is undiminished after Decoud's suicide—and the doctor's withdrawal and skepticism are more advanced than Decoud's—it seems more accurate to say that Conrad values the skepticism found in Decoud, but it can only reside in a figure strong enough to support it. Strength of character must be bonded to intellectual power.

Decoud's absence of real belief is evident in his failure to venture to the mainland, dangerous as that is, or make for open water on the slim chance of being picked up by a neutral craft. When the soul goes dead, alternatives no longer exist. One might infer that the moral affirmation for which Conrad is reaching is neither romantic love (Decoud's feelings for Antonia cannot overcome his sense of failure and impotence—he imagines her spurning him) nor political action (allegiance to his own Separation plan cannot check the descent to suicide). The great peril Monygham had lived through when he withdrew into the wilderness Decoud is unable to endure: "the crushing, paralyzing sense of human littleness, which is what really defeats a man struggling with natural forces, alone, far from the eyes of his fellows" (433). After twelve days on the Great Isabel, stricken with a withering sense of futility, Decoud dies from "solitude and want of faith in himself and others." This faith, a root impulse of ineradicable pride, is usually linked in Conrad to an exigency for redemption or a profound loyalty. It often expresses itself as fortitude, an unyielding effort to survive in the face of hopelessness. One sees it, for example, in Marlow's hanging on after his experience with Kurtz and the Congo. At times Conrad associates this strength with habits built up from arduous devotion to work, but Conrad's workers also fail in a crisis (e.g., Captain Archbold, Razumov as a student) and ultimately its source remains a mystery of character and spirit.

Isolation reveals that Decoud "was not fit to grapple with himself single-handed."

> Solitude from mere outward condition of existence becomes very swiftly a state of soul in which the affectations of irony and scepticism have no place. It takes possession of the mind, and drives forth the thought into the exile of utter unbelief. . . . Decoud caught himself entertaining a doubt of his own individuality. It had merged into the world of cloud and water, of natural forces and forms of nature. In our activity alone do we find the sustaining illusion of an independent existence as against the whole scheme of things of which we form a helpless part. Decoud lost all belief in the reality of his action past and to come. . . . He had recognized no other virtue than intelligence, and had erected passions into duties. Both his intelligence and his passion were swallowed up easily in this great unbroken solitude of waiting without faith. (497–98).

Decoud's standard of reason and passion proves disastrously wanting. Passion without principle or ambition has little staying power.

Ultimately, skepticism results in the annihilation of self. When the uncompromising intelligence has nothing external upon which to fasten, it will bore relentlessly inward. Mind becomes a weapon of penetration and reduction, eroding self-protective feeling, stripping away the illusions of egotism. Decoud has no reserves of resistance (he *has* led an empty life before he returned to Costaguana), and his inner hollowness echoes and succumbs to the void at the heart of Conrad's universe. Despite manifest differences, the effect of isolation on civilized Decoud makes one reflect on Kurtz in the interior. Consider this passage depicting Kurtz's corruption:

> Mr. Kurtz lacked restraint . . . there was something wanting in him—some small matter which, when the pressing need arose, could not be found under his magnificent eloquence. . . . the wilderness had found him out early, and had taken on him a terrible vengeance. . . . I think it had whispered to him things about himself which he did not know, things of which he had no conception till he took counsel with this great solitude—and the whisper proved irresistibly fascinating. It echoed loudly within him because he was hollow at the core. (131)

Kurtz's power lust, ingesting the world, breaks apart the boundaries of self, whereas mind turned against the self precipitates Decoud's collapse. "A victim of the disillusioned weariness which is the retribution meted out to intellectual audacity, the brilliant Don Martin Decoud, weighted by the bars of San Tomé silver, disappeared without a trace, swallowed up in the immense indifference of things" (501). Guerard comments that Decoud "achieves a kind of immortality in the commemorative medallion and Antonia's undying love,"[7] but one wonders at the nature of the extended homage had the truth of his death been known. Moreover, while Decoud's Separation plan is effectuated, Antonia's patriotism moves her to talk of reunion—to which Monygham objects that the material interests will never allow it (509). The effect of these details is not only to question posthumously Decoud's political acuity but to deepen the pessimistic future that Conrad prophesies for this world, to encourage a historical sense of the seeming futility of all political change in modern times.

Robert Penn Warren writes that "the last wisdom is for man to realize that though his values are illusions, the illusion is necessary, is infinitely precious, is the mark of human achievement, and is, in the end, his only truth."[8] Certainly, Conrad appreciates the pragmatic effectiveness and spiritual necessity of ideals, even when he shows those ideals to be illusions. Warren implies that man must accept limits to his deepest values and aspirations, a reasonable and civilized viewpoint. But this attitude does not offer Conrad a creative resolution; in his fiction, doubt about the truth of one's beliefs (their realizability, efficacy, personal worth, or higher right) undermines in disastrous and disabling ways the hero's capacity for action. Even Conrad's most articulate skeptics—Decoud, when he commits himself to rescue the silver by sailing with Nostromo, and Monygham, when he risks his life by betraying Sotillo—believe thoroughly, for their own reasons, in what they are doing while caught up in activity. If once Conrad's protagonists come to the knowledge that their values are illusions, the heart goes out of their response to life. What is involved is one's entire conception of self and the world. Disillusionment is profound and terrible; consciousness and lucidity, if achieved, rarely heal. If one survives, life now offers no hope, scant comfort, no remedy. Here, then, is Conrad's acute dilemma: after attaining tragic knowledge—moral penetration without illusion—how is one to live?[9]

IV

MONYGHAM has an importance in the novel not usually accorded a minor figure, being largely overshadowed in the critical literature by Decoud. The many elements in Monygham's character and history which reflect Conrad's preoccupations and meet with his approval point up his significance: the man's suffering, fortitude, and resignation, betrayal coupled with an unyielding sense of dishonor, his elevated feelings for an admirable woman, his sense of work, and mental acuity. It is primarily betrayal and the ensuing severity of his ordeal that make Monygham, not Decoud, the closer fictional kinsman to Razumov. Decoud has a range of freedom which Monygham's occupation and then terrible history deny him and which Razumov's Russian heritage, illegitimacy, and economic and political reality make utterly impossible.

Eighteen months of imprisonment under the harshest conditions, Father Beron's merciless interrogations, and breakdown under tor-

ture have marked Monygham for life. His lameness (cf. Jim's invalid-
ism after being struck by a falling spur) calls attention to an internal
crippling, a withering of emotion. The horror of that prison experience has stripped him of his social role, burned away sentimentality, left him ambitionless and with the bitter residue of guilt; at the
same time he has emerged with a tragic sense of life, sharpened in
mind, penetrating, and trenchant. There is a similarity in this pattern
with Marlow's growth of consciousness after his travail in the Congo.
Disillusionment prepares one to see the truth. Monygham never con-
templates suicide because of his degradation in captivity, and Conrad
always respects this gritty spirit of endurance, a quality lacking in
Monygham's intellectual peer Decoud. Despairing of men and civilization, and tormented by an anguished sense of personal failure,
Monygham upon release exiles himself for years in the wilds, wandering with Indian tribes in the interior, both hiding from the world
and disowning it. Though he survives, he does not heal. His bleak
attitude toward life stems in part from the crushing sense of human
littleness that grew upon him as he struggled alone with natural forces
during these years, an effort which impressed him with a perspective
of human insignificance in the cosmos (433). When he reappears,
hardened by deprivation, expecting nothing for himself, existence is
devoid of meaning. Living in penury and courting social disappro-
bation certainly reflect his disillusion and misanthropy, but they also
seem to express a form of self-willed penance. His refusal or inability
to be sociable suggests the pattern of a man still vexed by guilt. No
one judges him for his past deed, but an acute consciousness of lost
honor, though aberrant by the world's standards, dominates his
character. To describe Monygham, as does Hay, as "the realist, whose
only quirk is an exaggerated notion of his own fraility,"[10] is to dis-
count the importance of guilt in Monygham's life and to overlook,
by dealing inadequately with the treatment of guilt in the doctor, a
stage of development in this prominent Conradian theme. In the
eyes of the respectable, he is a "man careless of common decencies,
something between a clever vagabond and a disreputable doctor."
"So much defiant eccentricity and such an outspoken scorn for mankind seemed to point to mere recklessness of judgment, the bravado
of guilt" (312).

Unlike the usual pattern with Conrad's betrayers (e.g., Kurtz, Jim,

Nostromo, Leggatt, Razumov), Monygham immediately owns to guilt and suffers remorse, whose effect in Conrad is devastating. Remorse is just touched upon in Kurtz, but he relapses into delirium and dies soon after his one instance of moral illumination and self-judgment. Jim and Nostromo could not endure the corrosiveness and self-repudiation of remorse, for their unreflective egotism is essential to their strength. Once Razumov admits his guilt in betraying Haldin, confession and extreme punishment follow necessarily. Remorse has stripped Monygham of egotistical claims, and because he accepts responsibility, the fictional emphasis is not on the problem of unconscious guilt but on living with guilt without hope or expectation of redemption. Practical-minded Charles Gould "disapproved of the doctor's sensitiveness about that far-off episode of his life," considering it a kind of morbidness (408), but for Conrad it is imperative not to absolve oneself from responsibility, not to forget or rationalize, regardless of the world's tolerance or indifference. Redemption, if at all, does not emerge from forgiveness but from continued struggle with conscience. Personal integrity counts for more than community acceptance; indeed, without self-respect, reputation seems like imposture. Monygham is taken up by the Goulds and made chief medical officer of the mine when it "became apparent that for all his savage independence he could be tamed by kindness." He is given the opportunity to regain social place through work, and because of his chivalrous regard for Emilia, a sense of purpose grows in serving her.

Given the outrage inflicted upon him, Monygham might have understandably turned criminal or revolutionary. It is a measure of Conrad's political and moral conservatism that Monygham desires neither revenge nor social reform. Rather, the virulence of that experience is internalized, searing him emotionally and intellectually, so that all his battle is with himself. Monygham never considers himself a victim, even in part, driven to betray under the ravages of torture. Adversity, injustice, the abuses of power are for him the given of reality. Having lived through the worst, he can confront the starkness and the evil in life without falsifying or recoiling. His toughminded resignation embraces an awareness of the futility of hope, a cynicism regarding human motive, a tolerance for a corrupt status quo because to him change for the better is illusive. In its stoical aspect, Monygham's attitude reflects Conrad's mask, his habitual stance, a willed resistance; in Monygham's misanthropy is projected an extreme to which Conrad's skepticism, with its necessarily contracted emotional range, could carry. The darkest side of Conrad's skeptical detachment, untempered by humane feeling or romantic possibility, is most evident in *The Secret Agent*. Monygham scoffs at the engineer-in-chief's appreciation of the spiritual value of activity, dismissing idealization as "self-flattery." "I put no spiritual value into my desires, or my opinions, or my actions" (318). Yet the doctor is capable of idealizing his disgrace (no "realist" would allow himself to be so affected by a past misdeed) and of risking his life, not out of self-preservation or political conviction but because of an exalted love for a married woman.

Monygham has not sought redemption, but perhaps because of his suffering, consciousness, and courage Conrad grants him a qualified though definite success. The mine has given him purposeful activity and a measure of recognition, yet it is only in the aftermath of the fighting—his participation is brave and critical—that his recovery of self-respect becomes internal and effective. Playing the traitor to Sotillo, "abhorrent to his nature and terrible to his feelings" (439), repeats and redeems his original betrayal. However, in Conrad's ethical hierarchy, the stature of Monygham's conduct has limitations. His allegiance to the Concession grows out of dedication to Mrs. Gould, the mine becoming equated with her. "This illusion acquired force, permanency, and authority. It claimed him at last! The claim, exalted by a spiritual detachment from the usual sanctions of hope and reward, made Dr. Monygham's thinking, acting individuality extremely dangerous to himself and to others, all his scruples vanishing in the proud feeling that his devotion was the only thing that stood between an admirable woman and a frightful disaster" (431). Loyalty rigidifies into fanaticism. Locked into this state, he evinces no sympathy for others, being indifferent to Decoud's fate and quite ready to use Nostromo for his own ends when the Italian reappears miraculously after being presumed dead. Undeniably, the physician's part in the Sulaco events demands nerve and clearheadedness under the utmost risk. While his effort is not egotistical, it is undertaken in a spirit of self-sacrifice mingled with abasement (in contrast to self-affirmation); furthermore, he is motivated not by the independence of moral conviction but by reverence for another. What, one wonders, would Monygham do, if anything, had there been no Emilia?

Though Monygham does not represent Conrad's highest expression of integrity, he is the only substantial character in *Nostromo* to come out well (Mitchell is a patent object of satire). Conrad rewards his man with the recovery of self-esteem: his nightmares of Father Beron almost completely disappear, he is promoted to Inspector-General of State Hospitals, dressing now with austere formality, and he is permitted a deeper intimacy with Emilia. Conrad pays final tribute to Monygham's discernment by having him speak the impressive judgment on the material interests, an assessment which is given authorial weight in the novel.

> There is no peace and no rest in the development of material interests. They have their law and their justice. But it is founded on expediency, and is inhuman; it is without rectitude, without the continuity and the force that can be found only in a moral principle. Mrs. Gould, the time approaches when all that the Gould Concession stands for shall weigh as heavily upon the people as the barbarism, cruelty, and misrule of a few years back. (571)

But at the same time Conrad recognizes a destructiveness to Monygham's quality of mind, a compulsion to unmask that is also reductionist, that strips away illusion but also withers the possibilities attendant upon illusion without offering consolation. In seeking to ferret out Nostromo's shameful secret, Monygham would tear away the last shreds of his vanity, reduce the Italian, as he, Monygham, was once reduced, to humiliation and despair, diminish him to a fool and a thief. Of the daring and resourcefulness of the man, now dying from Giorgio's gunshot, who rescued all by his Cayta ride, of the earned reputation that would be irrevocably besmirched, the doctor cares little. Monygham's drive to expose, here cruel and inimical, fed by his own impulse for self-vindication, defers to Emilia's compassion and more human standard, the spiritual dimension wanting in Monygham.

V

NOSTROMO is Conrad's definitive consideration of romantic heroism. Entering the novel at the peak of his powers, fully achieved, Nostromo is an older Jim, a man in his element with no guilty past, no failure to mar self-confidence or infect consciousness. Jim's yearning for adolescent glory, the dazzle of heroism, is settled into an adult form of vanity in the Italian, and whereas splendor and acclaim were implicit in Jim's ideal self-conception, they are the very stuff of Nostromo's life. In their intrepidity, the French lieutenant and Stein afforded a mature corrective to Jim, and many individuals—Pépé, Barrios, Fathers Romàn and Corbelàn, and Monygham, among others—serve as foils to Nostromo in behaving courageously without being vain; they act out of duty, idea, love, heedless of widespread appreciation or the glitter of fame. Nostromo has none of Jim's callowness or self-absorbed dreaminess; he has the practical leadership qualities of action that are not developed fully in Jim, resoluteness, self-reliance, resourcefulness, competence in the face of danger and hardship. In this regard, he resembles Leggatt, and Nostromo's mile swim to the mainland after sinking the lighter adumbrates Leggatt's two magnificent swims for freedom. One feels that had Nostromo been challenged by the *Patna* crisis, neither his wits nor his heart would have faltered. Where Jim's notorious leap can be said to have created him and to have made possible a troubling romantic achievement incompatible with the maritime service, Nostromo's one partial defeat in the silver mission, more subjectively perceived than actual, begins a process of decline which Nostromo is unable and unwilling to resist.

Improvident, the seaman on perennial leave, Nostromo is the unencumbered male gambling away and giving away his wages, but, even here, his attitude toward money serves to enhance his self-image; he wishes to be and be known as magnificently independent, above measuring and counting, the generous overseer of his domain. He trusts the future to take care of itself, and with his attributes one is inclined to agree with him. His dread of impoverishment, which Teresa works up in him, is related to vanity, not to a fear of material survival. Nostromo is not a man to be reduced to pauperism. It is the idea of poverty's disgrace which he finds unbearable, the depersonalization and the deprivation of an admiring populace, a fear of losing his uniqueness. Despite his adopted family, Nostromo is more isolated, more proudly aloof than Jim. Because the Capataz has no sympathetic confidant and helper, no Marlow or Stein, the effect of Teresa's belittlement is all the more telling. Teresa scolds him for his neglect of monetary gain. "She was practical, and he seemed to her to be an absurd spendthrift of these qualities which made him so valuable. He got too little for them. He scattered them with both hands amongst too many people, she thought. He laid no money by. She railed at his poverty, his exploits, his adventures, his loves and his reputation" (254). An "intimacy of antagonism" exists between this mother surrogate and the orphan she had encouraged years ago to jump ship. Teresa is in part a nagging voice of conservatism and family values. She had always nursed the hope of securing in him "a friend and defender of the girls," perhaps a husband to Linda, and a companion to Giorgio because of her precarious health. Clearly, a domestic Nostromo is impossible. Marriage and the urban milieu are constricting and unsympathetic to the romantic side of Conrad's imagination.[11] At the same time Teresa understands intuitively that Nostromo's real interests do not lie with the Goulds, a truth Nostromo comes to accept later with galling resentment.

Teresa's sickbed request that Nostromo fetch a priest is less a seeking of religious consolation as life ebbs than a testing of her hold on him, a coercive wile incited by jealousy. Though Nostromo's refusal is assured by the urgency of his own mission, his disbelief in priests, and the seeming uselessness of the errand, the opposition of principle between them is reemphasized. Vanity and misplaced allegiance to superiors prevails at the cost of family claims. The melodrama of this deathbed scene gives an ominous import to her utterance:

> But do you look to it, man, that you get something for yourself out of it, besides the remorse that shall overtake you some day. . . . Get riches at least for once, you indispensable, admired Gian' Battista, to whom the peace of a dying woman is less than the praise of people who have given you a silly name—and nothing besides—in exchange for your soul and body. (256)

As he leaves her, she delivers a judgment that carries the power of an inspired curse: "They have turned your head with their praises. They have been paying you with words. Your folly shall betray you into poverty, misery, starvation. The very leperos shall laugh at you— the great Capataz" (257). Her prophesy strikes the vile image of his worst fears, the possibility he cannot face. (One is reminded how often in Conrad another's words have an extraordinary impact. Consider, for example, Brown's uncanny exchange with Jim, which forces the Patusan lord to back off.) Nostromo's dumbstruck retreat before Teresa's speech foreshadows his cringing downstairs before Hirsch's suspended corpse in the custom house; Hirsch is his fear objectified, a Nostromo debased, shrunken, lost. Equating poverty with disgrace is common enough, but in Nostromo it underlines his deification of fame and extreme vulnerability to ridicule. If identity is bound up utterly with image, loss of repute is a death blow, regardless of financial condition. Brierly committed suicide at the *possibility* that he might dishonor himself. Teresa's pronouncements, reinforced by Monygham's animosity and sardonic disparagement, come to haunt Nostromo with the force of accusation. And Monygham, jeeringly though unwittingly, echoes the dying woman's advice when he offers Nostromo his idea of the right bargain to be struck in this perilous venture: "Illustrious Capataz, for taking the curse of death upon my back, as you call it, nothing else but the whole treasure would do" (259).

Adrift in the gulf, Nostromo is unusually restive, determined to make this exploit the most famous and most desperate of his life. Decoud is right in having perceived that the Genoese "would have preferred to die rather than deface the perfect form of his egoism" (301). Such disfigurement must follow if the affair falls short, and it is for this reason—not for an understanding of the mission's political and economic importance—that Nostromo would have slain Hirsch. An inflexible ego-ideal constitutes a closed system. Driven to live up to an exalted self-concept at every opportunity and so confirm identity, the hero must satisfy those terms again and again in the name of conscience. Each triumph generates pressure for another. Failure is implicit in such compulsion, whether from miscalculation, impulse, self-doubt, fortuity, illness, age. If the hero is incapable of moral growth, extreme experience will precipitate collapse or degeneration. Despite the mishap with the transport, the undertaking is partly successful, having kept the silver from enemies. But by imposing subsequently on Nostromo a radical alteration of circumstance, forcing insecurity to surface, and causing the emergence of thought, the gulf episode sets in motion his downward drift.

Having deposited Decoud and the treasure on the island, returned to the mainland, and slept for half a day, Nostromo awakens "with the lost air of a man just born into the world" (411). The vocabulary of this rebirth sequence has an allegorical ring, an explicitness which insists upon the transforming effect and moral finality of the gulf experience. Reviving to the disappointment of a patient vulture, the fatigued swimmer mutters aloud, "I am not dead yet." But the old Nostromo of spontaneity, decisiveness, generosity, thoughtlessness, and easy confidence is no longer possible. What is significant is that this damaging change is not the result of guilt, for Nostromo has not yet committed a crime. Any dismay he feels over Teresa is aroused by his sense of abandonment, failure, and disorientation, and Conrad's ironic tone indicates the shallowness of that guilt:

> The magnificent Capataz de Cargadores, deprived of certain simple realities, such as the admiration of women, the adulation of men, the admired publicity of his life, was ready to feel the burden of sacrilegious guilt descend upon his shoulders. (420)

Events have compelled an inwardness in Nostromo which is as alien as it is devitalizing. The Italian senses that something is desperately wrong, but its nature escapes him. Rationalizing his plight: "A man betrayed is a man destroyed" (420) (in dramatic context, note how lamely Nostromo's conclusion compares with Razumov's "All a man can betray is his conscience"), Nostromo cannot see how his compliance with the *blancos*' demands amounts to personal responsibility. Though he begins to sense the folly and emptiness of his vanity, he still fears derision inordinately and will never outgrow his vanity. Isolation is unnerving, and "he was as ready to become the prey of any belief, superstition, or desire as a child" (417). Dislodged from his previous existence, he begins to see things differently, though, of course, reflection for him serves to ensnare rather than clarify. An immediate need for solitude and secrecy forces him out of his element, and this displacement robs him of his individuality.

Conrad knows that a romantic Nostromo cannot survive consciousness and modernity. In effect, Nostromo is killed by the old world and its code. At the same time, Conrad must pit him against his great tests of solitude and conscience. The weakness of the novel's close, essentially the consequences of Nostromo's theft, stems largely from Conrad's solicitous regard for his character, which acts to dilute Nostromo's suffering, and from the insufficiency of Nostromo to meet the demands of Conrad's tragic vision. Moreover, the theft is not a violation of a high order for Conrad, and as a form of betrayal it remains relatively safe for Conrad in the sense that remorse can be kept at a distance. Conrad's acknowledgment of the inadequacies of romantic individualism and his enduring affection for what Nostromo represents result in flawed compromise. For example, while the rough edge of consciousness begins to emerge in Nostromo, Conrad spares him clarity and hence its lethal impact; and while this errant son is punished, Conrad denies his death any heroic coloring. Nevertheless, Conrad goes farther than he did with Lord Jim in having Nostromo live on after willingly betraying the community and, more importantly, his self-conception. In a sense Nostromo answers the question of what would have happened to Jim had he not chosen death in Patusan: unresolved guilt, gradual and humiliating decline without opportunity for redemption. It is this debasement, symbolically a withering and relinquishment of romantic possibilities, that is so painful for Conrad.

Exposed and vulnerable after the gulf adventure, Nostromo might stumble his way to Emilia (Charles is Montero's prisoner) and report the truth. But what happens to him in the custom house, another of Conrad's brilliant face-to-face encounters, where Nostromo's fears catch him by the throat and Monygham seizes upon him as an instrument of rescue, has the effect of preparing the ground further for Nostromo's eventual crime. When the startled Monygham asks the identity of the slinking figure in the custom house, Nostromo answers, "A cargador." In that protectively anonymous reply is Nostromo's shame and sense of lost individuality. The sailor mistakes the suspended body of Hirsch for a living person, and in fleeing from it, he bumps into the doctor. Monygham is a correlative of Hirsch, and Nostromo's lurid, inflamed imagination exaggerates but little in seeing Monygham as a malevolent spirit. The claustrophobic, darkened interior heightens the sense of entrapment, conspiracy, and menace. Instinctive adversaries, the mordant intellect who disdains self and status and the active man of exceeding self-confidence who overprizes reputation, these two lock into confrontation, mutual suspicion mingling with need, their dialogue tense with misapprehension and calculation. Nostromo despises Monygham for his erstwhile destitution, a hatred based on the foreboding that he may become what the doctor once was. Badly shaken for the first time, caught up against his will in the whirlwind events of revolution beyond his understanding, Nostromo experiences that possibility as a tangible reality, as an ordained future already closing in. Teresa's prophesy "looked as if it would come true very quickly. And the leperos would laugh— she had said. Yes, they would laugh if they knew that the Capataz de Cargadores was at the mercy of the mad doctor whom they could remember, only a few years ago, buying cooked food from a stall on the Plaza for a copper coin—like one of themselves" (465). This image of damnation tyrannizes Nostromo. Conrad must convince us of the intensity of Nostromo's dread as a means of establishing motivation for his later decision to steal, a defiance of Teresa's curse of poverty. Going to investigate the "shadow" upstairs which incited Nostromo's flight, Monygham says to him, "Do not go away yet, Capataz." "Go away where?" answers Nostromo (426). This remark reappears, though with far more dramatic impact and a sharper sense of inescapability, as the devastating "Where to?" that Mikulin addresses to Razumov in *Under Western Eyes*. Nostromo is jolted to discover that Hirsch has also been resurrected. A fatal emissary destined to ensnare the living, Hirsch works a perverse revenge on both his would-be slayer Nostromo and on his frenzied murderer. Here the Conradian irony turns in on itself: Hirsch, the very figure of perfidy in his animal fear, has deceived Sotillo inadvertently by his gasped-out, bits-and-pieces account into believing that the lighter and its passengers were lost, though the colonel insists that the silver was not on board. Monygham's acceptance of this misinformation reassures the guiltily suspicious Nostromo, but it leads him deeper into an insidious subterfuge. In his own way, the doctor will continue the betrayal of these two victims of the silver initiated ironically by Hirsch.

The doctor's devotion, "absorbing all his sensibilities, had left his heart steeled against remorse and pity" (438) so that his attitude toward Hirsch is one of cold curiosity, a detached puzzlement as to why the tortured man was shot. This same absence of human concern extends also to Nostromo, alienating him further, feeding his class resentment and conviction of being abused. That sustaining, vital sympathy that Marlow offers Jim, that the captain and Leggatt share with one another, is denied Nostromo at a crucial moment. Isolated as he is, the Capataz expected the continuance of Monygham's flicker of interest in what had happened to him, "which, whether accepted or rejected, would have restored to him his personality—the only thing lost in that desperate affair. But the doctor, engrossed by a desperate adventure of his own, was terrible in the pursuit of his idea" (434). It is worth noting that Monygham never asks Nostromo directly about the shipment, assuming it went down in the accident. Given an attentive regard, one wonders if Nostromo would have revealed or hinted at the truth or if he would have met such a straightforward question with a lie. Conrad's method is to have Nostromo slip passively into falsehood and corruption. Overlooking Nostromo's agitated strangeness and throwing on him the mission to Barrios, Monygham indicates that in a gamble for time and to keep the enemy camps separated, he will misdirect Sotillo to the Great Isabel, a disastrous prospect for the Capataz, who still takes sole responsibility for the ingots. Quick-wittedly, Nostromo offers the pretense that the silver was sunk deliberately offshore. The doctor embraces the plan enthusiastically, but when Nostromo speaks aloud next, referring patently to Sotillo, he is pronouncing a personal sentence of doom as he well knows:

> There is something in a treasure that fastens upon a man's mind. He will pray and blaspheme and still persevere, and will curse the day he ever heard of it, and will let his last hour come upon him unawares, still believing that he missed it only by a foot. He will see it every time he closes his eyes. He will never forget it till he is dead . . . did you ever hear of the miserable gringos on Azuera, that cannot die? Ha! ha! Sailors like myself. There is no getting away from a treasure that once fastens upon your mind. (460)

And all the while Hirsch broods over the pair like a silent commentator, an intimate, imparting his pervasive air of treachery to the proceedings. On a frenzied impulse, Nostromo bolts for the town with the vague intention perhaps of reporting to Don Carlos. But catching up to the irresolute man, Monygham forbids him, "fiercely, almost beside himself with the fear of the man doing away with his usefulness for an imbecile whim of some sort" (462). Monygham's aroused intelligence does not fail him in this emergency, as he strikes all the right arguments to enlist the distraught sailor. He insists Nostromo would be betrayed if he entered the town, tempts him again with the prospect of glory, and soothes his distress over Teresa's death by urging him to enter the Casa Viola where Giorgio grieves alone. The irony here is that while Monygham manipulates Nostromo into performing his most important act of heroism, unknowingly he draws him away from Decoud and closer to his ruin.

Even after his legendary ride to Cayta, while on Barrios's rescuing ship, Nostromo still has the intention of producing the silver. In his procrastination, of course, lies a growing temptation. "Barrios, talking with Nostromo, assumed that both Don Martin Decoud and the ingots of San Tomé were lost together, and Nostromo, not questioned directly, had kept silent, under the influence of some indefinable form of resentment and distrust. Let Don Martin speak of everything with his own lips—was what he told himself mentally" (493). This passivity hints also at a want of moral standard. The marvelous detail of the lighter's dinghy come eerily to meet him has that touch of the significantly coincidental, that sense of a waiting opportunity which draws one to a line of action seemingly prompted by circumstance and secret desire. So well does Conrad evoke Nostromo's situation and psychology that his decision to claim the fortune is neither unexpected nor craven. Fashioned by a superstitious imagination and disenchanted vanity, Nostromo's justification is not a product of calculation or greed. "First a woman, then a man, abandoned each in their last extremity, for the sake of this accursed treasure. It was paid for by a lost soul and by a vanished life. . . . He had made up his mind that nothing should be allowed now to rob him of his bargain" (502).

Once Nostromo determines to steal, he damns himself to an imposter's role, forcing a split between image and self. The Italian's violation differs from the usual in Conrad in being willful, surreptitious, and unambiguous, the resolute grasping of an open temptation. Nostromo has been seduced into the deed not compelled, despite his fear of beggary. The deliberateness of the transgression and the choice to continue in his duplicity mean that guilt is conscious and constantly reinforced. Neither Jim nor Leggatt comes to a mature acceptance of guilt for his sea crime, and though this warding off must exact its toll (Jim's avoidance ultimately proves fatal), a steady erosion of inner strength does not occur. In flight from unresolved conflict, Jim still has the will to pursue his dream, however gropingly, and Leggatt can swim bravely toward a grim and uncertain future.

However, in Nostromo no defenses are possible to check the disintegrating effects of a widening psychic disunity: self-estrangement, loss of wholeheartedness, the ebbing of self-respect.[12] But because Conrad does not press down on his protagonist, Nostromo's suffering is neither convincing, moving, nor interesting. In practical terms, the continued availability of the silver nullifies any possibility of redemption, but on a deeper level, renewal is impossible because Nostromo is incapable of moral growth. Helpless to rid himself of the treasure and without public opinion, conscience, or inner pride to spur him to restitution, the romantic Nostromo declines in shabby and vulgar ways, pedestrian in an ill-fitting London suit, reverting to his original and prosaic name Captain Fidanza, cadging cigars, and attending unsavory political meetings. The love triangle and complications are the stuff of popular sentimental fiction.[13] To resort to this kind of plot contrivance indicates not merely an imaginative lapse, but also, I would suggest, the difficulties Conrad has in letting go of Nostromo within the confines of an already long novel, of delivering the mortal blow to his character. The pat execution of justice by a near-blind Father Viola is clumsy symbolism, a melodramatic and ineffective resolution. To make the shooting accidental seems to imply an authorial desire to avoid responsibility for the death. Conrad's strongest impulses and best art insist that punishment have the logic of self-punishment, proceed from the dynamics of self and not result from an outside agency. Just this absence of stress on inner forces is a predominant characteristic of the inferior later fiction.

To compare the fates of Jim and Nostromo is at once to recognize the inferiority of Conrad's handling of Nostromo's death. One is never persuaded of its inevitability or necessity. Neither individually nor in aggregate do Nostromo's questionable acts constitute offenses that are most charged for Conrad or that represent grievous moral issues. "Deserting" Teresa and Decoud is not in the realm of the immoral; moreover, these acts involve choices which do not bring dishonor upon the Capataz. Theft and a passionate love, whose clandestine nature and not its occurrence makes it a betrayal of "family" expectations and duty, hardly warrant capital punishment. One recognizes Teresa's aggressive and critical voice in Linda, and the younger girl is presented as more desirable physically and temperamentally. The Giselle entanglement is at worst somewhat shameful. No measurable

economic or political loss to either the company or the country registers because of Nostromo's illegality, which is not to condone em-
bezzlement that is undamaging to the public. More importantly, the
Italian is not responsible for the deaths of others as is Jim in Patusan
(Monygham's forced accusation, one recalls, led to political murders),
and certainly Jim's *Patna* dereliction is more reprehensible ethically
and more indicative of cowardice than is Nostromo's grand larceny
carried out ignobly. Jim gains stature—albeit ambiguous—by his willed
retribution; Nostromo is killed fortuitously and at the nadir of his
career. At the climactic moment, the old Garibaldini is far less imposing than Doramin, even while Conrad's aversion to these dis-
chargers of duty is suggested by their aged and rigid monumentality.
Furthermore, Jewel's bitterness, her justified charge of desertion, is
more substantive than Linda's cry of devotion, especially because
Nostromo's betrothed knows of his infidelity. And while it is true that
Jim's death freezes him into heroic form, untouched and untouchable, whereas Nostromo is humanized at the end, a figure of pathos
as he confesses to Emilia, this difference, indicative of Conrad's more
mature view of romanticism, proves detrimental artistically. Conrad
tries to grant his expiring Capataz a measure of dignity. But Nostromo's "glance of enigmatic and profound inquiry" as he refuses
silently in his last moments to denounce Monygham to the pale pho-
tographer or to grant his wealth to this "hater of capitalists" to be
used against the rich, while appropriate morally and a final gesture
of disdainful aloofness, carries neither the weight nor conviction of
Jim's "proud and unflinching glance" as he falls dead. The very ambiguity implicit in Jim's death was its strength, an ambiguity which
suggested that for Conrad issues were still open; no such complexity
obtains in Nostromo's case.

Emilia's lie preserving Nostromo's reputation, coming as it does in
this slack denouement, lacks the power, richness, and thematic integration of Marlow's white lie to the Intended which it resembles.
The cost and necessity, both personal and collective, of Marlow's
falsehood give it substance, but Mrs. Gould's lie, more an expression
of propriety and her weary disillusion than a moral statement, registers as unsatisfying and sentimental. An unfallen Nostromo seems
to prevail in memory, but the restored Monygham survives, his voice
silenced by Emilia's intercession. Both the Christian emphasis and

the note of falsity are troubling, as if Nostromo has triumphed over Monygham by default. Conrad does not espouse Christian thinking, and he is too honest a novelist, too rigorous a moralist, to back off from the truth as he knows it without his art suffering, as it does here. If the crime were exposed, Nostromo's renown would be tainted but not destroyed. In some quarters, the theft would even add posthumous luster to this man of the people. Were Charles to learn of the theft (the treasure is lost regardless because Emilia stopped Nostromo from divulging its location), a form of justice might be served in driving home to him the silver's evil influence. However, Conrad seems intent on underscoring the utter estrangement between husband and wife and Charles's death-worship of the mine, an obsession which seals him off from any possibility of spiritual recovery. In any event, Conrad chooses not to risk Nostromo's repute (or a longer novel) for this declaration of truth. Instead, truth has been bartered for a compassion compromised by a lie. Nostromo's confession unburdens, Emilia's forgiveness shields, but these do not reestablish Nostromo's integrity.

The logic and conviction in Conrad's theme of betrayal point inescapably to redemption through remorse and punishment. Nostromo dies unrepentant, unredeemed, and without heroic stature. The idealized Emilia serves here as a protective screen, for in holding off Monygham, she spares Conrad from the darkest implications of his tragic vision. Clearly, romanticism cannot withstand the onslaught of knowledge. Conrad is unable to relinquish finally the claims romanticism has on his imagination. Unscathed by Monygham's withering glare, Nostromo's remembered image becomes Conrad's nostalgic tribute, the residue of an imaginative inspiration but not an abiding moral ideal. Monygham, though, is a force of reality and mind that can only be met by uncompromising truth rooted in moral and intellectual courage. One senses that for Conrad no illusion, no sympathy, no outside intervention, no work, no community can spare one from the ravages of nihilism and the facts of a tragic existence. Razumov and autocratic Russia are waiting to be evoked. Nostromo, then, marks the effective end of the Conradian romantic hero, a fictional idea carried to its limit, and with his demise a vital phase of Conrad's art is played out.

CHAPTER FIVE

"The Secret Sharer": Affirmation of Action

I

IN LATE November, early December 1909, Conrad put aside the unfinished *Under Western Eyes*, which he had been working on for the past two years, and began "The Secret Sharer," completing it in less than a month.[1] He then resumed *Under Western Eyes* and brought it to an end; the typescript is dated "End. 22 Jan. 1910."[2] Even more than the overlapping period of composition, internal evidence suggests a special relationship between the short story and the end of the novel.[3] For psychological and creative reasons, to relieve the burden of consciousness and find release and inspiration in self-affirming action, it was essential for Conrad to compose "The Secret Sharer" before he could finish the unsparing, artistically inevitable *Under Western Eyes* to which his major themes point. The Russian novel is a resolution of major proportions, a working out in ultimate terms of fundamental conflicts, particularly the themes of betrayal, guilt, punishment, and redemption. In "The Secret Sharer," Conrad's treatment of these concerns is open-ended, resulting in a future for the two comrades that is problematic but to which Conrad extends a deserved hope. In *Under Western Eyes* Conrad carries these fictional ideas to their limit, stamping them with a sense of conclusiveness. Furthermore, Conrad realizes in Razumov his maturest conception of integrity, central to which is growth of consciousness, a quality noticeably absent in the captain. The unsentimental but questionable affirmation which closes the sea tale is better understood if "The Secret Sharer" is seen as the romantic counterpart to the tragic *Under Western Eyes*. Other elements in these contiguous works contribute to this sense of complementarity: the maritime sphere and the problems of leadership as against the urban milieu and the realm of politics; upholding a direct appeal for trust in contrast with Razumov's cowardice and infidelity to Haldin. But the most telling difference is in their respective endings: youth advancing confidently into the future set against Razumov's terrible futurelessness. Two controlling factors in "The Secret Sharer" help account for Conrad's moral attitudes as well as this concluding note of hope, a rare feature in Conrad's best art. There is an absence of the usual Conradian skepticism, primarily because of Conrad's use of an "unintellectual" first-person narrator; by not exerting ironic or moral pressure on his spokesman, Conrad lessens the severity of his tragic vision. (Only Archbold suffers its full brunt.) And second, an impulse which flows from this absence, Conrad places a decided emphasis on courageous action to the subordination of moral consciousness.

At the outset of his initiatory journey, understandably anxious because of first command, the novice is profoundly unready for leadership. Beneath a posture of youthful assurance exist inexperience, doubt, a vague sense of self, and an imagination given to romanticizing and abstraction. Despite some resentment and suspicion, the crew cannot know and the captain himself cannot appreciate just how dangerously vulnerable he is. Protective self-ignorance, reinforced by vanity, is matched by a naiveté of outlook; he thinks reality safe and reasonable, the sea and men predictable and moderate. Other details more strongly call into question his moral fitness. It is hinted that this choice of a career of presumed moral simplicity is partly an evasion from the snares, duplicity, and uncertainty that the captain ascribes solely to the land. He is defensive about how he received his commission ("In consequence of certain events of no particular significance, except to myself, I had been appointed to the command only a fortnight before"),[4] and this guarded tone suggests his uneasiness that factors other than deserved merit, the usual steady rise up the ranks, were instrumental in his assignment. (Leggatt was taken on through connections, and suspect circumstances were involved in the placements of Marlow and Kurtz in "Heart of Darkness.") As he confesses to Leggatt, "I had been appointed to take charge while I least expected anything of the sort" (122). Callowness is associated invariably with an unpreparedness for critical experience, but Conrad does not view such unreadiness leniently or absolve one from accountability because of youth. When do the weaknesses linked to callowness become the character flaws in an older person? For example, when does an adolescent self-absorption become blinding egotism, unsophistication of mind become willful ignorance or irresponsibility, inexperience become a calculated evasion of significant encounter? Conrad uses the unpreparedness of his heroes to set the stage for a radical test of character. In unreadiness, all past safeguards, of ordinary consciousness, of habitual responses, of vanity, prove unavailing; life seems to expose and bear down unerringly on just those facets of self which make the risk of failure most acute. For anyone with claims to integrity, the ensuing conflict is inescapable and total, and Leggatt's coming plunges the beginner into just such a trial.

Conrad provides numerous signs that Leggatt is to be regarded as a symbolic manifestation of the captain's unconscious, his being a physical double both suggesting and reinforcing unconscious connections.[5] The night setting, the captain in sleeping garb, his mood of reverie and introspection evoke the world of dreams. Prompted by a feeling of strangeness, he dismisses the anchor watch and assumes the post himself, an unusual disruption of established routine which startles the crew. His unaccountable behavior is responsible for leaving the rope ladder over the side, the link of communication which brings Leggatt to him, and in this way the captain may be said to have invited his visitor.[6] Leggatt remarks that the captain seemed to have expected him. The swimmer appears to rise from the depths of the sea, a universal symbol of the unconscious, to the surface, to conscious life. Feeling weight on the ladder, the commander peers over the rail and sees an eerie, ghostly-glowing shape. "He was complete but for the head. A headless corpse" (102). And the observer's head completes the figure. Just from their initial exchange of words, the captain senses a "mysterious communication" established between them, suggesting an intuition of a special kinship. Leggatt is a messenger, a "legate," an emissary of the unconscious come to confront the apprentice with unrealized aspects of himself, a harbinger of the captain's future, an inspirer who helps promote the becoming of identity.

In the sense that the visitor corresponds uncannily to the wished-for male image, one might say that the captain has dreamed Leggatt into existence. To act forcefully when it matters most is what the tyro questions in himself, admires and envies in his confederate. On one level, as Guerard argues, Leggatt is "the embodiment of a more in-stinctive, more primitive, less rational self,"[7] but simultaneously he is an ideal possibility for the captain, an inspiration and example, an epitome of leadership.[8] As the stranger announces his name, the nar-rator thinks, "The voice was calm and resolute. A good voice. The self-possession of that man had somehow induced a corresponding state in myself" (110). Later, the captain admires Leggatt's ability to plot his escape from the *Sephora* during his six-week captivity: "And I could imagine perfectly the manner of this thinking out—a stub-born if not a steadfast operation; something of which I should have been perfectly incapable" (117). Significantly, when escape does oc-cur, Leggatt describes it as his giving in to a sudden temptation as he dived off the ship and was in the water before he fairly made up his mind. The captain's marked agitation after the steward's near-discovery of the stowaway in the bathroom is in sharp contrast to Leggatt's steady self-control, a bearing that causes the observer to marvel "at that something unyielding in his character which was car-rying him through so finely" (145). That composure under duress can hearten another sympathetically is a truism, not at all unfamilliar to Conrad's pages. A simple expression of this effect, for example, is in *Typhoon*. Fearfully shaken during the hurricane, Jukes experi-ences a resurgence of confidence and self-belief at Captain Mac-Whirr's steadfastness, his conviction that the way to get through the worst seas is to run with the wind, to face it and keep a cool head.

In *A Personal Record*, Conrad describes a decisive episode during which the sight of "an ardent and fearless traveller" infused his de-moralized adolescent self with renewed spirit. On holiday in 1873, the fifteen-year-old Conrad saw a vigorous Englishman marching through the Furca Pass as he sat nearby dejected before his tutor's arguments against his taking to sea.

> Was he in the mystic ordering of common events the ambassador of
> my future, sent out to turn the scale at a critical moment on the top
> of an Alpine pass, with the peaks of the Bernese Oberland for mute

and solemn witnesses? His glance, his smile, the unextinguishable and comic ardour of his striving-forward appearance helped me to pull myself together. . . . I had been feeling utterly crushed. It was the year in which I had first spoken aloud of my desire to go to sea. (41)

Conrad's epithet for him, "the ambassador of my future," even in name suggests Leggatt, another manly envoy come unexpectedly to inspire a youth in his vocation. In the memoir, Conrad gives an imaginative and life-shaping importance to the whole Furca Pass incident, rounding off the experience by noting that eleven years later he became a master in the British Merchant Service.[9]

Both Leggatt's calm and capacity for spontaneous action are vital to the commander's ideal conception of himself. "There are to a seaman certain words, gestures, that should in given conditions come as naturally, as instinctively as the winking of a menaced eye. A certain order should spring on to his lips without thinking; a certain sign should get itself made, so to speak, without reflection" (140). Experience and habitual performance help create the naturalness of professional conduct; such unity implies surety of self, a confident relation to the inner life. Obviously, as with the captain, dissociation from one's interior being can induce debilitating conflict. At the same time, Conrad suggests that stalwartness and self-command draw upon instinctive vitality, just as the demonic and savage have their source in primitive impulses. "The same strung-up force which had given twenty-four men a chance, at least, for their lives, had, in a sort of recoil, crushed an unworthy mutinous existence" (138). This amoral energy can help carry a man through in a crisis, but it can also cause self-abandon. Leggatt strangles the mutineer in a "fit of temper" as a huge sea wave smashes over the pair, the chief mate's engulfing aggression paralleling the fury of nature. Leggatt has a forcefulness that can break through all restraint, and Conrad implies that the unconscious has the power to move a man into actions both brave and lawless.[10] One intellectual advance from earlier works in Conrad's conception of the unconscious is a recognition of its beneficial potential, acknowledging it as a source of strength and not (as most notably in "Heart of Darkness") as something primarily to be feared and repressed in civilized man, associated with the illicit and self-destructive.

On the face of it, the captain's protection of the escapee seems to present an acute conflict between Conrad's private and public values.

An outlaw's appeal for trust and another chance is set in direct opposition to maritime law. That the captain acts out of "psychological
(not moral) reasons" (133) is entirely convincing. Not all commentators accept this line of argument. Consequently, the apparent merger
of Conrad with his persona and what this effect means about Conrad's attitude toward Leggatt (the narrator takes no moral stance)
leave many critics uneasy, if not baffled. For example, Donald Yelton
writes that "the narrator does not pronounce against Leggatt's act;
and I do not find that Conrad, by any device of irony or multiple
perspective, implies any moral judgment beyond the judgment (or
suspension of judgment) of the narrator."[11] Daleski states that critical
readers cannot "unreservedly accept the captain-narrator's easy con-
donation of him [Leggatt]; but this is the judgment that the author,
limited here to the point of view of his narrator and not having any
recourse to irony, would appear to want us to make."[12] The question
is not made any less perplexing by the observable impression that
conduct motivated by sympathetic identification *seems* like an expression of moral endorsement. What more could the captain do for Leggatt, one asks, if he sanctioned his actions throughout? An additional
knot: if one grants an incapacitated moral sense during the actual
experience, one must note that in recapitulating the events, the captain offers no moral perspective. Drawn to Jim, Marlow could crit-
icize him simultaneously.

Though the young officer might not consider himself bound to
confront the moral dimensions of his conduct, Conrad by no means
evades those issues, which are dealt with implicitly. Doubtless, the law
would not recognize the captain's psychological reasons as exculpa-
tory, compelling as they are. However, Conrad forces us to weigh
the question of illegality (harboring a fugitive) and reckless endan-
germent (the Koh-ring venture) against the possible consequences if
the captain had not become Leggatt's ally. To say nothing serious
need have happened is to disregard Conrad's terms: the novice's romantic misperceptions and self-ignorance, crew members verging on
disrespect (slack authority led to the fatal eruption on the *Sephora*),
inner defect (Archbold breaks after thirty-seven years of service,
Leggatt kills a man), and nature's ferocity and treacherous calm. To
the charge that the narrator is irresponsible in not getting to know
the crew and ship, it can be answered that such intimacy is impossible
in his present condition with Leggatt on board. And even if the run-

away had not appeared, familiarizing himself with his command would
not reach his depths of unease, would not rouse in him the urgency
to act upon the real danger posed by his deficient knowledge. The
strain of concealing Leggatt exacerbates a divisiveness he had from
the outset, but to the crew he seems as peculiar as when he first
boarded. He performs minimum duties and gets by because nothing
demanding is called for. Enforcing a mood of indeterminacy and
anxious waiting, the oppressive heat and faint breezes in the gulf
invite the reader to suspend judgment as the captain retreats in-
wardly.[13] Leggatt brings matters to a head, so to speak, and as a result the captain gains a psychological preparation and sense of crisis
which enables him to initiate the Koh-ring maneuver and carry it
through with disciplined authority.

II

THE IDEA of acting for psychological and not moral reasons is
critical to the story and helps clarify other important encounters
of a similar nature in Conrad. For example, I see no moral content
in Jim's release of an armed Brown. Whatever ethical judgment
Jim may have been capable of is corrupted by sympathetic identification with Brown, by a need to repress guilt, by cowardice and
egotism. Similarly, to argue that Razumov aids Haldin initially out
of "compassion"—which carries an aura of the moral—is to over-
simplify and sentimentalize Conrad. Had Razumov a genuine belief in his convictions, clear-sightedness, and courage, he could—
without regret and with unassailable justification—have ordered
Haldin from his room once the assassin began explaining himself.
Sympathetic identification, invariably with the outcast or law-
breaker, derives its considerable power and complexity from unconscious connections. Indeed, when intellectual or moral affinity
is absent, as in the Jim-Brown and Razumov-Haldin pairings where
trust is misplaced, sympathetic identification can have the gravest
consequences. Fidelity to the double has to do with remaining
faithful to aspects of, and possibilities intrinsic to, oneself. The real
difficulty arises when the leading character of the two harbors a
corrupt element of self, e.g., unresolved guilt, masked cowardice,

a form of morally ambiguous romanticism which he has not examined or is not prepared to repudiate. However, no such complication obtains in the captain's situation because he has not yet
failed. The violative act in Conrad is a crime exposed to the public
which simultaneously is an offense against conscience, often repressed. This condition does not apply to the captain. He has no
reservations about his confederate (the story, however, dramatizes
a moral distinction); trust is honored; and though the captain's
psychological stress is increased drastically, the end result of the
relationship is mutually beneficial. Leggatt's astonishing physical
likeness to his rescuer makes the latter's identification with him
immediate and serves to reinforce deeper bonds. Conrad is here
making explicit the key feature of sympathetic identification: intense involvement with a part of self. One has only to recall Marlow's profound affinity for Kurtz to realize that physical similarity,
while having a decided impact, is not essential to such a relationship. Leggatt and the captain are "doubles" regardless of looks.
Nevertheless, their external resemblance, insisted upon by Conrad, reminds us constantly that the captain is in the grip of a compelling and unrelieved fascination, a mixture of passivity and wonder, which nullifies autonomy. Conrad's emphasis on doubleness
is an important strategy for persuading us that moral judgment
does not enter into the commander's conduct, encouraging us not
to question his untroubled conscience over union with a fugitive.[14]

Links of kinship exist other than appearance and background. I
have already discussed Leggatt as the captain's ideal. An immediate
point of communion is their common situation vis-à-vis their respective ship's company. The captain's position of being an isolated
outsider regarded with suspicion is pushed to an ugly extreme in
Leggatt's case. Though appointed through family influence and not
engaged directly by Archbold, Leggatt faces an outright antagonism
that has less to do with resentment engendered by nepotism than
with the threat he poses to the unofficial governing arrangements
because of Archbold's lapsed authority. "He was afraid of the men,
and also of that old second mate of his . . . a gray-headed old hum-
bug; and his steward, too . . . a dogmatic sort of loafer who hated
me like poison, just because I was the chief mate. No chief mate ever
made more than one voyage in the *Sephora,* you know. Those two

old chaps ran the ship" (118–19). Having his wife on board is a
Conradian telltale of Archbold's unfitness. In such circumstances,
Leggatt is substantially the responsible power of the ship. Flinching
before the need to use the foresail is the dramatic culmination of
Archbold's eroded leadership. Conrad's case against the aging married seaman is damaging indeed. The captain's grey-striped sleeping
suit, a duplicate of which he gives Leggatt, resembles a convict's uni-
form and evokes the wearers' outcast and adversary status, implies
that the captain is becoming increasingly a prisoner of his own fears,
and signifies that in fact, if not in conscience, he is guilty of breaking
the law. Up against the reality of a wrecked career, Leggatt is living
out the captain's deepest insecurities. Protecting the symbolic failed
self becomes a means of succoring himself in defeat, of warding off
his own potential ruin, and of drawing sustenance from the living
proof that spirit can remain unbroken despite crushing odds. Increasingly, the captain's fate, like his identity, begins to merge with
that of the other. Obviously, discovery of the stowaway would all but
destroy the captain professionally and expose to official inquiry his
self-misgivings, but more subtly, if Leggatt cannot gain reprieve, this
shutting down may in some essential way foreclose the future for the
captain as well, strike fatally at his root sources of being. Both their
destinies, it turns out, hinge on Koh-ring. In embracing the pariah,
the captain has unconsciously begun to shape the crucial opportunity
for himself, the decisive act of mastery and courage.

What the protagonist sees as injurious in his bonding with Leggatt is not the violent inner conflict it induces, the near-insanity
of a divided nature, but rather his excessive dependency, which
he recognizes as a form of cowardice. When Leggatt advances the
idea that he must depart, the captain exclaims, "You can't!" Immediately, however, he catches himself and reflects:

> I felt suddenly ashamed of myself. I may say truly that I under-
> stood—and my hesitation in letting that man swim away from my
> ship's side had been a mere sham sentiment, a sort of cowardice.
> (146)

The sentiment was false because self-indulgent, a clinging need for
security and comfort springing from the fear of facing his ordeal
alone. That wishes and feelings can take on the psychic equivalent

of deeds is unarguable, but here Conrad implies that shameful feelings can have a private reality which is the moral equivalent of a deed. Such an extreme standard contains a streak of fanaticism, an exigency for a purified, heroic self. To sustain this lofty self against the assaults of experience is all but impossible. This romantic pursuit, however, is a rich imaginative inspiration for Conrad, and he follows it to its end point (cf. the fates of Marlow in "Heart of Darkness," Jim, Gould, Nostromo, Haldin). Part of the urgency behind the daring hunt for land breezes is the captain's need to redeem himself from this lapse into cowardice. "It was now a matter of conscience to shave the land as close as possible — for now he must go overboard whenever the ship was put in stays. Must! There could be no going back for him" (154). There was never any doubt as to Leggatt striking out for freedom, and I think the imperative here is self-directed, an exhortation to make the necessary rupture, to authenticate self by severing the incapacitating dependency he has developed for his twin.

If one contends that the Koh-ring enterprise is "irresponsible,"[15] by the same token Archbold is "overly-cautious" in not ordering the foresail set during the hurricane. To shun risk would have doomed the *Sephora*. There is for a captain a critical area of initiative and personal decision beyond rule book procedure and conventional thinking. And even where suitable methods have been codified, the commander must be able to discern their applicability and bring himself to follow them. With resignation unthinkable, the story argues that the captain's uncertainties, a threat to reliability and performance, can only be overcome through action. It goes without saying that a leader's miscalculation about himself or lack of self-faith jeopardizes the men under him. For the terms of selfhood the captain wants and obviously needs, there is no prudent course: to let matters stand would doubtless worsen his condition and further strain ship morale; to remain alert for an eventual danger rather than force the issue would be psychologically wearing and a dubious strategy for confronting life. The captain is primed now, the moment is there to be seized. Desire converges with opportunity, aspiration rushes against fear. Conrad implies that in the field of action, with a participant caught up in the immediacy of experience, a standard of moral scrupulousness cannot be pressed.[16] Abstract right in this instance will not serve. The issue is not one of calculated pragmatism since the captain can hardly be said to have acted with premeditation. What the story rewards and what a favorable outcome hinges on are values of heroism, disciplined self-mastery, spirited engagement, virtues of a warrior's code. This same problem of reaching a moral judgment as to the protagonist's means and ends, his apparently "egotistical" behavior during the heat of charged experience, is evident in Gould's threat to explode the mine in *Nostromo*. Both episodes are similar in that necessity and success seem to outweigh moral reservation.

Fear grips the captain as he drives the ship landward, but with a Leggatt-like aggressiveness, he presses nearer, determined that the ship will weather. What begins as a controlled risk develops rapidly into a crisis. As Porter Williams, Jr., emphasizes, with the ship only half-about in her turn windward and poised near the rocks, the newcomer does not know whether she has gathered sternway. Without such knowledge, he is in effect blind and cannot give an informed command.[17] This eventuality was of course unforeseen. What prevents shipwreck is the success made possible by the "favorable accident" of the floppy hat. During the emergency, the whiskered and sneering mate, a double to the bearded Archbold—tenacious, rational, dogmatic—and reminiscent in diminished form of the insolent mutineer who challenged Leggatt, is reduced to whimpering helplessness, paralleling Archbold's funk. This moment of peak stress for the captain, hovering on the precipice and utterly alone in his position of responsibility, when panic could sweep the crew and absolute discipline is crucial for survival, duplicates the conditions faced by Leggatt in the gale. Shaking the mate's arm (Leggatt shook his antagonist like a rat) to jar him from his fear and compel obedience to orders gives some indication of the "strung-up force" within the captain, but paralysis rather than violent outburst seems the greater danger for him. So formidable are the demands of Conradian selfhood that one must undergo a test where all is at stake, an ordeal that brings one within a hair's breadth of the horror, to the very gates of darkness (Erebus) that lead to the hell of unredeemable moral failure. With the peril of Koh-ring scant yards away, the captain spots his white hat and reacts with that part of himself which is aware, responsible, disciplined. "And I watched the hat—the expression of my sudden pity for his mere flesh. . . . behold—it was saving the ship, by serving me for a mark to help out the ignorance of my strangeness" (158). Self-pity not moral approval prompted the captain to give Leggatt his hat to shield him from the tropical sun because he suddenly imagined himself suffering the exile's desolation. The return of the hat implies a *moral* separation between the two selves, though a profound affinity cannot be denied. The man who had once "lost his head" must leave behind the hat, which becomes in context an emblem of conscience. Leggatt must return as he came, a "headless corpse," a being primarily physical and instinctual. When the captain thrust his hat on Leggatt, he thought of it as a protective headpiece. Conscience of course is that part of consciousness which protects a man from losing restraint. Because he pulls back at the critical point, the narrator earns the name of captain, fusing self with professional role.

Needless to say, Conrad's attitude toward Leggatt is far from simple. Whereas Jim blamed circumstance and his own unpreparedness, Leggatt does not throw off responsibility for homicide, but he will not permit himself to be judged by the community, especially a parson father who could not possibly understand. Though the idea of standing trial is repugnant to Leggatt, the factors arrayed against a strong legal defense seem well-nigh insuperable: the crew's hostility to the outsider, the more so now with one of their own killed, the extreme circumstances which make for fragmentary and unreliable reporting, Leggatt's setting of the foresail without due authorization, as well as Archbold's character, distinguished record, and sense of his own faintheartedness if not malfeasance. These considerations have the effect of gaining favor for the criminal and his decision to choose exile. However, Guerard warns against an undue sympathy for the man, cautions against identifying Conrad's attitude with Leggatt's strong-willed egotism. "Essential (from an officer's point of view) is his [Leggatt's] contempt for law, his feeling that innocence and guilt are private matters."[18] Nevertheless, my own conclusion is that guilt, judgment, and punishment *are* ultimately personal concerns for Conrad, and I appreciate the powerful resistance, often taking baroque forms, which this authorial conviction generates in his art. As with Jim, Conrad does remove Leggatt from the service and send him out of the civilized world, but in this story and elsewhere, what emerges as fundamental to Conrad's morality is the preeminence of conscience over the claims of external authority. Conrad's attitude expresses an unyielding individualism, even if it be noted that conscience for him is more exact and terrible than the law. On this score, Conrad's work prompts troubling reflections. For instance, one can accept legal and even personal responsibility for a crime without feeling remorse: one's sense of guilt may be shallow or unconscious or one may feel one has not debased conscience. The illicit need not correspond with one's sense of the unethical. Guilt may be felt for neurotic reasons, for reasons which society would not deem immoral, or for hidden reasons not linked causally to any one act. This terrain is Kafka's rather than Conrad's but certainly relevant to any study of guilt. And most tragically in Conrad, conscience becomes the last measure of humanity in a country whose legal system is unprincipled, an instrument of politics. Nevertheless, from a social point of view, particularly in a democracy, individual morality superseding collective values is dangerous and arbitrary. It will be observed, however, that none of Conrad's protagonists/violators escapes punishment, though the effective penalty is not through law or public disapproval.

Clearly, psychological accuracy and moral content are Conrad's absorbing interests rather than legal or public accountability. One may suppress guilt like Archbold or distance oneself physically from its reminders like Jim or refuse institutional judgment like Leggatt, but no man with claims to integrity can truly escape its effects. Part of Conrad's complex moral judgment can be inferred from the presence of guilt feelings in his characters. Throughout the interview with the captain, Archbold mumbles, appears ashamed and distressed, recites the introductory facts "in the manner of a criminal making a reluctant and doleful confession," is desperately evasive about his own and Leggatt's role during the storm. Granted, we perceive Archbold through the eyes of someone who sides emotionally with Leggatt, but nothing contradicts, even by implication, this description of Archbold or Leggatt's version of the *Sephora* events, as there does, say, the captain's sure optimism at the end. If the reader does not accept the accuracy of the narrator's depiction of Archbold, his entire narrative becomes hopelessly tainted. Although the old skipper will be spared a trial, he appears guilt-ridden and self-condemned, an index of his failure and of the limitation—in its conventionality and rigidity—of the world he represents. His last years marred, deprived of the consolation of a faultless career, he cannot be a free man. Leggatt's disappearance into a wilderness "unknown to trade, to travel, almost to geography" differs from Jim's flight in that unlike his fictional predecessor, Leggatt is not seeking redemption and escape from disgrace. This parson's son does not feel dishonored—note his forthright manner of presenting the details compared with Jim's tortured account of the *Patna* experience to Marlow. The victim and the circumstances of the crime may help explain Leggatt's want of self-reproach, but to condemn him for not feeling remorse is presumptive; one cannot impose an obligation to feel. The absence of remorse is part of his character. One might say, in providing a neutral description, that Leggatt is not a man of thought, that what we see of him makes moral growth beyond him. At the same time, Conrad is abetting his survival by sparing him the inner rift that saps Jim and seems to afflict Archbold. Conrad wants us to see Leggatt's exile as simultaneous punishment and opportunity, as both payment and emancipation.

III

COLORED by a young man's triumph, the ring of affirmation which closes the tale is emotionally stirring, but as an interpretation of events, the narrator's words require qualification. For reasons having to do mainly with the completion of *Under Western Eyes*, Conrad needed to win a confident rendering of life's possibilities that did not dilute his more deeply felt tragic knowledge. Dark elements verging on the tragic exist in "The Secret Sharer" as background, as implication, as a sufficient force of opposition to compel a more sophisticated, comprehensive, and sober perspective than that offered by the speaker. And while cause for self-assurance and promise is cut back, nevertheless, a basis for hope remains justified. That the text yields a less sanguine view of things than the conclusion would warrant is readily apparent. The sheer accident of the bobbing hat, far from being a flaw in the work, is its essential point. Daleski protests that the fortuity of the hat's appearance is a weakness, "for it makes his achieve-

ment of knowledge too much a matter of chance—and it turns the
highest kind of seamanship into a tightrope of contingency."[19] But
to ponder the meaning and implications of this luck at the very edge
of disaster is enough to shake one considerably, to chill the elation
in any sense of victory. And when chance's role in this near-death
escape is added to other unsettling realities—the fact that Archbold
broke after a lifetime of laudable service, that in personal terms his
one failure annuls an entire career and will spoil his remaining days,
that Leggatt can be both hero and murderer, that the amoral, destructive, and unpredictable inhere in nature and human nature—
a sense of trust in the world and in oneself is undercut sharply. The
terms of existence register as harsh, precarious, and threatening. No
guarantees are possible, no safeguards are sufficient. Anxiety becomes a constant of being, and a permanent element of uncertainty
relating to all action enters consciousness.

Attuned to this skepticism, one can pursue a more "Conradian"
reading of the narrator's final pronouncement: "[M]y secret
sharer . . . had lowered himself into the water to take his punishment: a free man, a proud swimmer striking out for a new destiny"
(159). A painful and enduring deprivation, Leggatt's exile means to
be lost to family and country, to leave behind a blackened reputation
as murderer and suicide that he can do nothing to repair. Knowing
that the captain has understood him, that his story will be remembered with sympathy as he has told it, is a heartening source of consolation. Slander and obloquy will inevitably attach to his memory
with no one to speak in his name. The importance of upholding reputation (here, through the loyalty of a confidant), especially when
made vulnerable through questionable failure, withdrawal, exile, death,
is a recurring motif in the author's work and prompts one to reflect
on Conrad's distress at those accusing Polish voices, real and internalized, that continued to assail his "defection." Leggatt's fate means
also to be compelled to adopt a new name and identity—never without its costs for Conrad—to move into a future outside the bonds
of white civilization (perhaps a symbolic way of Conrad bidding
farewell to his exotic romanticism, burying it with Leggatt's "suicide"), to be denied the fraternity of the craft and the attainment of
his chosen profession. With this stark reality before Leggatt, how is
one to understand the assertion that he is a free man with a virgin

future? Elsewhere in Conrad, the notion of freedom never escapes the grip of his skepticism. As Marlow says of Jim's yearning to start afresh: "A clean slate, did he say? As if the initial word of each our destiny were not graven in imperishable characters on the face of a rock" (*Lord Jim*, 186). The captain's "Impossible! You can't" to Leggatt's plan to go off the face of the earth echoes Marlow's reflection on Jim's hope to escape into a new life, though without Marlow's understanding of the impossibility of disowning the influence and deeds of one's past. By themselves, a change of place and name do not transform moral character; Leggatt carries memory and his ungovernable violence with him.

This much had to be said to correct any overstated optimism, but Leggatt's fate also contains promise. For those who rationalize wrongdoing like Jim and, in more complicated ways, Razumov, Conrad's method is to bring them to see the violative meaning of what they have done. If, as a matter of speculation, one were to place Leggatt in this pattern, the question arises whether he would be able to withstand emergent moral consciousness. Two factors in conjunction set him apart from Conrad's flawed heroes and lend support to the captain's hopeful projection for him: Leggatt's crime is not an act of cowardice (a point to be underscored), and he is thoroughly unromantic. Tough-spirited and tough-minded, he has none of Jim's callowness or the narcissistic weakness common to both Jim and Nostromo. Leggatt does not fear disrepute, poverty, or social neglect, and with some assurance one can envisage him establishing and maintaining a solid life in this remote region by his own efforts. At the same time, to give substance to the claim that Leggatt is a "free" man, a transgressor who has squared his accounts, Conrad must satisfy the demands of his artistic conscience for a higher sense of justice than legal prosecution. Punishment and redemption are integral to such demands. Leggatt's exile is sufficiently hard and exacting to warrant seeing it as punishment, though his suffering will not be the internal anguish of consciousness, conflicts engendered by guilt, self-scrutiny, disillusionment. However, with redemption the matter is subtle.

Conrad has split this theme and its resolution between two characters. Previously, with Jim and Monygham, Conrad grappled with this problem of winning integrity in the face of necessary punishment in a single figure, but in each case qualifications suggested an incomplete working out. In Conrad's terms, the crime must be redeemed by a reliving of an equivalent of the original deed and by an act of courage where once there was irresponsibility. In "The Secret Sharer" the chief mate's "legacy" is to inspirit his ally to rise up to his best self; in achieved captaincy, the initiate becomes an unfallen Leggatt. By living through a trial essentially similar to Leggatt's storm ordeal but by exerting restraint at the crucial instant where Leggatt lost himself, the captain has "redeemed" his double in the sense that the compulsive pattern is broken, the crime is not repeated. By suggesting redemption through the efforts of the captain, Conrad has taken the issue beyond Leggatt's subjectivity, for to the fugitive, his act does not admit of reparation, he suffers no psychic cleavage, and he accepts exile as punishment. Thus, Conrad would seem to have removed the need for redemption from Leggatt's future, and artistically the moral dimensions of Leggatt's case are settled within the story's confines. Like Marlow growing into an identity that has roots in Kurtz, becoming transfigured from seaman to "voice," the captain reincarnates Leggatt, who has died to the world. In both instances, a man capable of extremes bestows a legacy of spiritual paternity in that he is responsible for quickening to life a self in his own image latent in the other which emerges, however, as the morally stronger.

Conrad's granting favor to a pair of young men has much to do with his characterizing neither as a romantic egotist. Experience has cut through the captain's complacency and romantic glaze without the disillusionment that annuls self-image. A consciousness of leadership, not the pursuit of heroism or reputation or a transcendent private cause, is strong in both men. Duty compelled Leggatt to set the foresail, and later, as a prisoner, he chooses not to endanger the men on the *Sephora* by attempting a violent escape. Because the narrator's identity is bound to the values of the calling, the necessity impelling the Koh-ring challenge serves not individualism but maritime ideal.[20] By way of contrast, professionalism merged with egotism distinguishes Brierly. The surety won by the captain is the kind that is absorbed in the blood; he has it in reserve, a knowledge and capacity he can call upon in the line of duty. But he cannot be said to have reached maturity because he lacks developed consciousness, those attributes of mind Conrad associates with moral acuity.

Neither introspective nor probing, the quality of the captain's intellect stands forth in the direct simplicity of his narrative. It is without the reflective commentary, the groping for clarity, the note of hesitancy and anxious brooding that characterize Marlow's yarn in "Heart of Darkness." Such forthrightness reveals the untroubled mentality of a young captain just come into his own, markedly different from the moral philosopher Marlow of both the Congo story and *Lord Jim*. Using an uncomplicated first-person narrator of densely complicated material does more than heighten immediacy. There is no retrospective sense, no time gap between the original events and their recounting. In contrast, the effect of elapsed time in "Heart of Darkness" between Marlow's experience and its recital is important dramatically. The storyteller is substantially different from the man who underwent the journey; a breakthrough in consciousness has been painfully achieved, and this struggle for knowledge is felt to be actively continuing. However, one detects no intellectual growth in the captain. Conrad does not give his young hero time or cause to meditate. By sparing him the onset of thought, Conrad preserves the captain's victory and secures for himself the vital sense of youth winning out, of life opening, of spirited effort rewarded that emerges dominantly from the story. This romantic necessity afforded Conrad imaginative strength, consolation, and sustenance as he returned to complete the searing ordeal of *Under Western Eyes*, whose stark finality inflicted an agonizing toll on its creator.

CHAPTER SIX

Under Western Eyes: Integrity Achieved

I

CONRAD'S romanticism, specifically his belief in the redemptive and self-authenticating illusions motivating heroic action, is excluded rigorously and repudiated in *Under Western Eyes*. One reason for the success of this controlling feature of the novel is that romantic impulses find their disciplined outlet in "The Secret Sharer," the two works complementing each other in significant ways. Certain consequences bearing on *Under Western Eyes* flow from this complementary relationship. Conrad eliminates effectively the need for romantic solutions or compromises, which usually result in ambiguity, diffusion, retreat, or sentimentality. He is able to do complete justice to his tragic vision in a political context charged with his most intimate history. Because of Razumov's character and the nature of his transgression, the interrelated themes of betrayal, guilt, and integrity receive their fullest treatment and reach their most compelling climax in Conrad's work. For the first time Conrad dramatizes explicitly the willful betrayal of the double who appeals directly for trust. The extraordinary burden Conrad sets for himself, in addition to "the obligation of absolute fairness . . . imposed on me historically and hereditarily, by the peculiar experience of race and family,"[1] is to win affirmation in the face of guilt and consciousness. Razumov earns an integrity that satisfies Conrad's severest judgments and enables him to both honor his protagonist and grant him compassion. The terms of resolution can be no more exacting and final, implying as they do a renunciation of the world, the exhaustion of Conrad's belief in the self-affirming possibilities of action.

Western eyes may overlook the implications of Razumov's neglectful attitude toward political reality, but the danger posed by inattention is as urgent and grave as that posed by the captain's naiveté in "The Secret Sharer." What the newly-appointed skipper is insufficiently aware of and ill-equipped to meet—the destructive and unexpected in nature, problems of winning command—would be appreciated for the most part by a British audience. More subtly, a like fictional situation obtains in *Under Western Eyes,* where the protagonist's response to a menacing world is callow and inadequate. Conrad places a student with an exorbitant need for security in a milieu where neither inconspicuousness, prudence, "law-abidingness," nor industry can make up for the absence of legal guarantees central to a democratic society. Conrad's use of an English narrator who does not grasp that Razumov's mild neutrality is evasive and has helped breed an unjustified sense of security tends to disguise further the seriousness of Razumov's unconcern with establishing a principled political position for himself. Seeming to endorse Razumov for moderation in the midst of passionate divisions, the teacher records that with Russia plagued by internal dissensions, Razumov "shrank mentally from the fray as a good-natured man may shrink from taking definite sides in a violent family quarrel" (11). But this mental shying away is an intellectual shortcoming reflective of an uncreated self, for the novel insists that personal identity is inseparable from politics. Ordinary and diligent, Razumov confines himself to a life of cautious routine. Sociality for him is not a benefit worth cultivating, but his inclination for solitude is not pronounced or abnormal. "He worked at home in the manner of a man who means to get on, but did not shut himself up severely for that purpose. He was always accessible, and there was nothing secret or reserved in his life" (6–7). Aside from a bland cordiality with university people, all his energies are absorbed in work, seen as a way of making a name for himself. A distinguished name would carry special significance for this obscure Russian, an illegitimate son "with no Razumovs belonging to him anywhere." Namelessness or lack of a "proper" name in Conrad often suggests a moral uncertainty of self. "Razumov was one of those men who, living in a period of mental and political unrest, keep an instinctive hold of normal, practical, everyday life. . . . his main concern was with his work, his studies, and with his own future" (10). In a tyranny, however, normalcy is an illusion; life is *more* precarious than Razumov assumes. Haldin's coming and its aftermath expose dramatically the moral challenge in such an environment that Razumov is unprepared to face.

Of critical importance is why Razumov does not order the intruder from his room once Haldin announces his deed. To claim for Razumov an act of compassion is simply to misread the text. Unconscious identification, distinctive of Conrad's psychological method and especially in encounters of apparent opposites, is at work here. Clearly, Haldin is no homicidal ruffian, and while there is always the chance that the assassin might be provoked to violence if dismissed, such a reaction seems out of character and Razumov never considers it. Excruciating though his predicament is, entailing peril regardless of what he does, the possibility of banishing Haldin does exist. However, once the first few seconds pass—the decisive moment—Razumov seeks to master his dilemma by mind, but his secret ambivalence and profound fear of disruption and risk make his ratiocinations suspect. However much Razumov may seem to be "without choice," Conrad does not foreclose all options, which would remove personal responsibility and hence grounds for moral judgment. Razumov's passivity, a quality of softness, is meant to suggest callowness, an unfinished moral character. Razumov's good looks are slightly marred by

a peculiar lack of fineness in the features. It was as if a face modelled vigorously in wax (with some approach even to a classical correctness of type) had been held close to a fire till all sharpness of line had been lost in the softening of the material. . . . In discussion he was easily swayed by argument and authority. With his younger compatriots he took the attitude of an inscrutable listener, a listener of the kind that hears you out intelligently and then—just changes the subject.

This sort of trick, which may arise either from intellectual insufficiency or from an imperfect trust in one's own convictions, procured for Mr. Razumov a reputation of profundity. . . . By his comrades at the St. Petersburg University, Kirylo Sidorovitch Razumov, third year's

student in philosophy, was looked upon as a strong nature—an altogether trustworthy man. (5–6)

This "imperfect trust in one's own convictions" that the narrator imputes to Razumov with a matter-of-fact casualness reverberates with
import. While such a lack is not unusual in any student or young
adult and would not seem to amount to a glaring fault, nevertheless,
Conrad forces us to see this uncertainty as serious indeed. For Conrad, it is not merely a transitory phase in one's development, a for-
givable aspect of youth, but a moral flaw whose significance is high-
lighted because of a Russian context where politics dominates life.
Razumov and his generation are thrust early into a universe of few
choices and urgent pressures. In the concentrated world of *Under
Western Eyes,* one's political creed is one's morality, and ideas carry
the weight of deeds. To disregard or attempt to steer clear of politics
yet to establish one's ground, as Razumov tries, is a moral evasion
and is shown to be unworkable.

Startling and inopportune as is Haldin's appearance, his very presence (he is esteemed highly by friends) and opening words praising
Razumov flatter the lonely philosophy student unused to such attention. Habitually, Razumov shuns giving offense, skirts controversy
and confrontation, and his inability to say no ("He was liked also for
his amiability and for his quiet readiness to oblige his comrades even
at the cost of personal inconvenience" [6]) implies an unawakened
sense of self-importance. In avoidance and passivity for Conrad lay
irresponsibility, suggestions of cowardice, unformed conscience. It is
not entirely a stroke of fate, an ironic perversity, that Haldin should
seek out this particular acquaintance. Razumov's contemplative air,
solitariness, and self-effacement beckon, invite, and "win over" the
activist Haldin. Patently, Haldin is using Razumov, even if not with
conscious malice, though bound up with the single-mindedness and
crude formulations of his revolutionary thinking are self-serving cal-
culations as to Razumov's situation and absence of family ties. The
very lack of forcefulness and definition in the orphan allows Haldin
to appropriate Razumov's identity, to think of him in ways that take
scant account of his separate individuality, however elusive and indistinct. By affecting neutrality, by not forging and making known
his own convictions, Razumov remains without essential boundaries,
a passive entity, unresistant to others' romanticized and distorted

characterizations. In cultivating safety, Razumov inadvertently courts complication and misapprehension. He fails to take notice of the impression he, even he, makes on people. The subtle ways in which reputation, others' expectations and perceptions of one, bear on identity are a persistent concern in Conrad. The undeserved profundity and trustworthiness comrades attribute to Razumov recall the excessive goodness individuals confer upon Marlow in "Heart of Darkness," and the ready confidence people usually feel toward Jim and Nostromo. An ascription of inflated virtue can have consequences as grave as unmerited disrepute.

With utter assurance, Haldin details the assassination as if conversing with a brother, a sympathetic ally who understands and approves of all. Vanity often ensnares but rarely with such vengeance. Seething with outrage despite his welcoming demeanor, listening to Haldin instruct him on fetching Ziemianitch, Razumov himself wonders "why he had not cut short that talk and told this man to go away long before. Was it weakness or what?" (20). A hurried survey of his plight persuades him that his instinct is sound. But the drift of Razumov's thought, guided by the counsel of prudence, has a murderous underside:

> It was best to keep this man out of the streets till he could be got rid of with some chance of escaping. That was the best that could be done. Razumov, of course, felt the safety of his lonely existence to be permanently endangered. This evening's doings could turn up against him at any time as long as this man lived and the present institutions endured. They appeared to him rational and indestructible at that moment. They had a force of harmony—in contrast with the horrible discord of this man's presence. He hated the man. (21)

If all risk is anathema, then only Haldin's death can insure Razumov's security. The seeds of betrayal are already present. An unconscious attraction for his visitor also silences Razumov's protest. As the bold, vigorous youth, Haldin is the obverse and hidden side to the cautious, sedentary intellectual, the adventurous self beyond Razumov's capabilities but which he envies secretly. Just as Haldin romanticizes Razumov as the thinker ("Unstained, lofty, and solitary existences" [135]),[2] Razumov harbors an uncritical admiration for the strong, soldierly male. Conrad provides suggestive descriptions. Entering his room, Razumov spots the shape of an intruder. The man's

form "loomed lithe and martial" (14). Haldin's "supple figure, with
the white forehead above which the fair hair stood straight up, had
an aspect of lofty daring" (18). Realistically, Haldin is less the warrior
than an unsophisticated idealist resigned to martyrdom. In the novel's urban, political context, the heroic, active version of self is un-
realizable. By way of contrast, Sophia is determinedly unromantic, a
disciplined revolutionist and tireless worker, immune to vanity. That
an attraction for the venturesome and individualistic, elsewhere such
a vital, imaginative force for Conrad, destroys both Haldin and Razumov, is a measure of how far Conrad has come in curbing, if not
rejecting, the romantic side of his nature. Against Russian despotism,
romanticism is a fatal miscalculation. Razumov's idealization of male
power translates politically as a yearning for the authoritarian dic-
tator. In his frustration with Ziemianitch, Razumov seizes upon the
argument for the single Russian will. The tableau of a frenzied Razumov beating the drunken peasant suggests the Russian spirit of
autocracy, its traditional justification, and its ultimate futility.

The way Razumov's fear of being implicated with Haldin shapes
itself in his imagination, its intensity and theme of inevitable, unal-
terable ruin, betrays the influence of his orphanhood, his loneliness
and habits of avoidance, his ambition for a celebrated professorship:

> Razumov saw himself shut up in a fortress, worried, badgered, per-
> haps ill-used. He saw himself deported by an administrative order, his
> life broken, ruined, and robbed of all hope. He saw himself—at best—
> leading a miserable existence under police supervision, in some small,
> far-away provincial town, without friends to assist his necessities or even
> take any steps to alleviate his lot—as others had. Others had fathers,
> mothers, brothers, relations, connexions, to move heaven and earth
> on their behalf—he had no one. . . .
> He saw his youth pass away from him in misery and half starva-
> tion—his strength give way, his mind become an abject thing. He saw
> himself creeping, broken down and shabby, about the streets—dying
> unattended in some filthy hole of a room, or on the sordid bed of a
> Government hospital. (21)

The teacher-narrator, drawn naturally to a student and would-be academic and linked further by his English sensibility attuned to Razumov's conservatism, accepts unquestioningly the diarist's fears. Primarily in the St. Petersburg section of the novel, his voice is an
important means of building up sympathy for Razumov.

A simple expulsion from the University (the very least that could happen to him), with an impossibility to continue his studies anywhere,
was enough to ruin utterly a young man depending entirely upon the
development of his natural abilities for his place in the world. He was
a Russian: and for him to be implicated meant simply sinking into the
lowest social depths amongst the hopeless and the destitute—the night
birds of the city. (25–26)

Fear and helplessness frequently generate melodrama, a species of
distortion. Under despotism, the worst can happen and often does.
However, what is melodramatic in Razumov's projection lies not in
the impossibility of this sequence but in his fastening on *only* this
outcome, investing it with finality, and in his picturing himself as
unresisting and defeated. Here again in Conrad is the panic-struck
imagination prone to visualize crisis as catastrophe, to equate anticipated disaster with certain reality. One thinks of Jim's state of mind
before leaping from the *Patna* and Nostromo's fear of poverty and
ostracism. The French lieutenant, disciplined and unselfconsciously
intrepid, serves as a foil to Jim, and Monygham, who lives through
what Nostromo dreads, is fearless because guilt-ridden and without
egotism. In *Under Western Eyes,* Natalie, who will return to Russia,
and Sophia can stand as contrasts to an irresolute Razumov in their
courage against autocracy's might and in the respect they command
from Conrad. Their spirit stems from their versions of patriotism
and revolutionary faith, which demand self-sacrifice and renunciation of conventional social ambition. Natalie is fortified by her radiant vision of the future, and Sophia has the grit of a veteran sol-
dier. What Razumov cannot endure is the prospect of a life of
obscurity, which to him means waste and desolation. However un-
appealing, there is this obscure existence if one wants a measure of
freedom and does not wish to harm others: a moral life, in honorable
poverty. But to endanger one's own life to save a virtual stranger
and political adversary, to be willing to surrender secular ambition
and its rewards, to imperil one's future and the hope of gaining
prominence through one's talents, is to transform the nature of ordinary being, a Tolstoyan vision. For Razumov, a solitary intellectual,
without religious feeling or yearnings for community, this existence
is not merely intolerable but beyond conception, outside his realm
of values. By the end of the novel, however, Razumov is a changed
man.

Two responses to a ruptured life and futurelessness can be seen in Leggatt and Monygham, inhabitants of a more primitive and open world. As the officer swims to forbidding Koh-ring, naked and dead to human society, he has an unswerving faith in his capacity to endure and flourish by personal effort. Importantly, he is not shackled by consciousness or guilt, and his crime is neither cowardly nor willful. The obvious differences between Leggatt and Razumov point up Conrad's embrace of the resourceful, physical man and his deep uneasiness with the intellectual. Imagining himself barred from advancement and hemmed in by the police, Razumov envisions life as penury and abject decline. His fear resembles Nostromo's dread of impoverishment should he lose face, though the student has far more cause for alarm. For Razumov, the substance of identity resides in its outward, societal aspect, grounded in reputation ("Life is a public thing"; "The field of influence was great and infinitely varied—once one had conquered a name" [54,71]), but identity on such terms, as evident in Nostromo, need not have moral content. Monygham faces a desolate future lacerated by guilt; freedom is the beginning of his trial. One critical difference between him and Razumov is that implicitly the physician holds that what matters about self is not status but the primacy of conscience. Only after prolonged torment, imprisoned by hate, remorse, and falsehood, will Razumov come to stake his life on private terms of authenticity.

It is not at all self-evident in what sense Razumov's informing on Haldin is a betrayal of conscience. Razumov's justifications, even if self-serving, must be answered, and the five political statements he writes out in the aftermath seem to favor the regime. The matter is complicated further by Conrad's conservative leanings, which can lead one to identify Razumov's political creed and its implications with Conrad's own. Addressing this knotty issue, Guerard notes judiciously, "Even the betrayal of Haldin, seen in the context of Conrad's respect for law and distrust of revolution, could be said to correspond with certain authorial convictions. But only with convictions and only with certain of these. . . . Razumov . . . is (when he informs on Haldin) dramatized as committing a crime; he has violated the deepest human bond."[3] This essential human bond, referring to a Western ideal of humanity, is in the novel, however, not to be taken on faith as a moral absolute since Razumov resists this imperative fiercely. A secular injunction against murder might be stated thus:

to a morally sensitive and/or a wholehearted person, taking a life, even if that of an enemy, even if with society's sanction or in self-defense, is a wrong that strikes deep into one's being. The soul incurs a wound, though it need not be debilitating. That unconscious guilt eats at Razumov's insides is evident, but the remorse he comes to acknowledge at the end is no simple admission that he violated Haldin. One notes that he never feels compassion for the man.

If a murderer or political assassin comes unsolicited for help, one is bound legally to assist in his arrest. The issue remains relatively clear-cut if neither established friendship nor shared values exist between the pair. Circumstance never exonerates for Conrad, though he does not underestimate the extremity of such pressure. More, then, is demanded of an individual. Had Razumov gone directly to the police, he might have been on better terms with himself, and the moral case against him would be weakened. But ethical judgment in Conrad is always problematic, not least because of the dark nature of motive. One remembers the captain's claim that he aids Leggatt for psychological not moral reasons; isolation, an uncertain sense of self, and profound identification with the homicide make it impossible for him to act otherwise. Razumov understands at once that he and Haldin are political antagonists. So total is the political climate in St. Petersburg, so charged is the immediate confrontation for Razumov that there can be no question of his separating Haldin from his political role, if indeed such a distinction can be made. To the philosophy student, Haldin incarnates hated ideas, and it is the intellectual weakness in both Haldin's idealism and person, the absence of rigorous thought, that has led him to endanger Razumov so atrociously. Haldin's proclamation reveals to Razumov the futility of argument: "When the necessity of this heavy work came to me and I understood that it had to be done—what did I do? Did I exult? Did I take pride in my purpose? Did I try to weigh its worth and consequences? No! I was resigned. I thought, 'God's will be done'" (23). There can be no pardon for what Haldin has done to Razumov. Although Haldin is the same man who weeps because his bomb also slew innocent bystanders but who, out of political necessity, would do it again, he is no hardened ideologue. Once Razumov after returning reveals his biography to Haldin, a masked confession but also an assertion of who he is, the revolutionary feels no hostility, never damns him as a reactionary or czarist supporter.

However, what can never be overlooked is that the Russian system is lawless, so that all rational moral claims of the state are invalidated. Razumov craves order and stability, imputed invariably to strong government, but without justice, these qualities in themselves have specious ethical worth. The assassin may embody for Razumov the spirit of anarchy, but the state itself is terroristic. At the same time, if Razumov believed implicitly in the present form of autocracy, giving up Haldin would not arouse such conflict. Razumov holds to the logic of secular development and a reasonable, not mystical, belief in absolutism, whose preservation will prepare the way for the one great man of the future. Cognizant of the state's oppressive methods, unavoidable corruption, and unchecked use of power, even if he does not characterize the regime as evil, Razumov never considers himself liable to its disfavor. Although other criticism is brought to bear, it seems to me that what damns Razumov's act unequivocally for Conrad is its cowardice. Even after his botched errand to Ziemianitch, Razumov could still have expelled Haldin from his quarters despite his increasingly exposed position, but to do so now is utterly beyond him. Resourcefulness or "readiness" is not the point; what matters is courage that comes from integrity of being. Even if Razumov were capable of a more acute assessment of his reality and the tenuousness of all security in Russia, no premeditation or mental rehearsing could have readied him for Haldin. In his internal debates with himself, he never claims unpreparedness as the dubious excuse for not having dealt strenuously with Haldin, but he does rage for not knowing enough to fling the man downstairs. Though incomplete, his admission is more honest than Jim's protest that he was caught unawares on the *Patna*. The willful decision to betray exposes the cowardice implicit in Razumov's character and flows logically from his initial response to Haldin: "He had simply discovered what he had meant to do all along" (38–39).

It is true that Razumov's faithlessness is a breach of human solidarity, but he professes no allegiance to such an ideal. To say that his conception of the human lacks breadth and richness is to sum up the meagerness of his life, more a cause for pathos than condemnation. The text suggests, however, that Razumov's act against Haldin dishonors the spirit of patriotism. Alien as it is to him, Razumov never mocks Natalie's generous vision, an outgrowth of the heart but not the method of her brother's idealism. A vital idea of fraternity might have tempered Razumov's aloofness, selfishness, and insecurity; it might have restrained the fear that prompted him to purchase what he thinks is safety with another's life. But if solidarity is at all possible between these two, it cannot be founded for Razumov on brotherhood or nationality—his political aversion to Haldin is unbridgeable—but on a recognition that in their stolen youths they are common victims of a Russia which is crushing and unlivable. Razumov may sense this truth on his own behalf when he gazes profoundly at Spontini's "Flight of Youth," but he never grasps its larger meanings. Here, in shared victimization, is the basis for a moral connection, for the state, protector of the status quo with which Razumov identifies his welfare, does not serve him as he assumes. It is another telling argument that the secret affinity Razumov feels for Haldin, his buried romantic self, and the reality he creates by going to the carriage driver constitute a link to Haldin entailing some responsibility, however much Razumov would disown such an obligation. Complicity in the morally indefensible even while one maintains a virtuous self-regard is a familiar Conradian problem of conscience. Getting Ziemianitch, Razumov reasons, is a way of ridding himself of this horror with the least damage, but he knows he has compromised himself. Although the charge of complicity dogs him, Razumov never articulates the full significance of acceding to Haldin's plan, just as he never concedes cowardice in surrendering the utopist. This knowledge may be beyond his understanding, blocked perhaps by pride and the need for self-protection. Despite a conservatism which seems to ally him with the government, by logic and moral force Razumov's true position amounts to independence, a way of being, however, for which he has not yet the courage and clarity necessary for commitment. Whatever perplexities remain, approaching Ziemianitch means that Razumov has ostensibly taken sides, that is, he has broken with a valued independence. Likewise, in going to the authorities, regardless of his private view of the matter, he has also aligned himself. There are consequences to choosing sides which Razumov neither perceives nor will shoulder.

II

THE "scrupulous impartiality," "the obligation of absolute fairness" Conrad felt bound to sustain in his handling of Russian material was taxed severely in his treatment of revolution, that patriotic romanticism that doomed his father and in profound ways shaped Conrad's inner life. As much as Conrad the mature thinker abhorred armed rebellion, had he not left his homeland it seems more than probable that he would have followed his father, engaging in some reckless political venture. Even Najder, who debunks vigorously Conrad's autobiographical embellishments and personal myth-making, grants that the young Conrad may have been involved in gunrunning soon after his leave-taking.[4] The guilt so often attributed to Conrad may have as an element not merely the charge of deserting Poland, betraying his parents' sacrifice and ideals, but also the burden of survival. Hence, the abrupt departure at sixteen assumes the character of a second chance in that Poland would have undoubtedly spelled ruin or death for Conrad through some ill-advised act of insurgency. Aspects of Conrad as well as his father are discernible in Haldin. Edward Crankshaw theorizes that if Conrad had stayed in Poland, his only alternative to revolt would have been collaboration.[5] Barring outright assistance to the Russians, this description is perhaps too harsh to apply to all those difficult choices short of violence. Armed resistance is not the only patriotic response. However, a third desperate alternative exists, that of a strict and resolute independence, a version of nonactivism while speaking with a free mind. As Conrad knows, to stake out such an existence entails unremitting danger and requires exceptional personal qualities. Not to support the czarist government with demonstrations of loyalty, even if one is, like Razumov, not a dissenter, can be construed as treason. And with virtually no room for maneuvering, one must yet earn a livelihood. Nevertheless, this independence, central to the integrity Razumov attains finally, is the position that the mature Conrad seems to espouse. But to have embodied this stance had he remained in Poland would have been utterly impossible, given his character and the enormous pressures impinging on him. Though rare, such an independence is possible in a dictatorship, at least in our own day, but historical conditions are vastly different: the support of segments in the democratic West for

dissenters from tyrannies is more real; the acquiring and dissemi-
nation of information and the weight of international opinion are
definite influences; the prospect of cooperation between opposing
camps, primarily economic, is a tacit bargaining point. In the novel,
this independence is shown to be unlivable or, rather, achieved with
a morally regenerated Razumov crippled and dying.

With Ziemianitch useless, Razumov is plunged into Conrad's characteristic scene of trial: solitude, night, nature's enormity and pitilessness, here given a historical cast. Desperation is intensified by a
lifetime of loneliness.

> Razumov thought: 'I am being crushed—and I can't even run away.'
> Other men had somewhere a corner of the earth—some little house
> in the provinces where they had a right to take their troubles. A ma-
> terial refuge. He had nothing. He had not even a moral refuge—the
> refuge of confidence. To whom could he go with this tale—in all this
> great, great land? (32)

Seeking strength for what he desires but is fearful to articulate, Razumov turns to the physical fact of the land and to the idea of Russia.
Under this weight, before this "sacred inertia," human life dwindles
to insignificance. National salvation is identified with the need for
an omnipotent ruler, a belief that satisfies also Razumov's yearning
for personal safety. "For a train of thought is never false. The falsehood lies deep in the necessities of existence, in secret fears and half-
formed ambitions, in the secret confidence combined with a secret
mistrust of ourselves, in the love of hope and the dread of uncertain
days" (33–34). Driven to merge autocracy and messianism, Razumov
makes the leap from logic to mystical certainty; casting off the anxiety of doubt and responsibility, he reflects obedience when he thinks
himself most inspired. Hallucinating Victor's prone figure across his
path in the snow, Razumov concentrates himself and walks through
this ghost, intent on crushing an impediment, oblivious to what might
be a warning, a call. Once safely past, he declares, "I shall give him
up." Even after death, Haldin will continue to bar his way. "Betray.
A great word. What is betrayal? They talk of a man betraying his
country, his friends, his sweetheart. There must be a moral bond
first. All a man can betray in his conscience. And how is my conscience engaged here; by what bond of common faith, of common
conviction, am I obliged to let that fanatical idiot drag me down with

him" (37–38). His reasoning leads inevitably to the one conclusion. "He was firmly decided. Indeed, it could hardly be called a decision. He had simply discovered what he had meant to do all along. And yet he felt the need of some other mind's sanction" (38–39). Despite raising his decision to an act of conscience, Razumov has a hunger for confirmation, which testifies to the insufficiency of his rationalizations:

> Razumov longed desperately for a word of advice, for moral support. Who knows what true loneliness is—not the conventional word, but the naked terror? To the lonely themselves it wears a mask. The most miserable outcast hugs some memory or some illusion. Now and then a fatal conjunction of events may lift the veil for an instant. For an instant only. No human being could bear a steady view of moral solitude without going mad. (39)

These powerful words evoke Decoud's plight on the Great Isabel. At the breaking point, Decoud kills himself; Razumov's betrayal of Haldin is moral suicide in that he strikes at his own deepest humanity, an act that only later he recognizes as self-destructive.

Central to Conrad's theme of integrity is the isolation and independence forced upon the moral agent, most absolute in Razumov's prolonged ordeal. No sympathetic confidant, no necessary and beneficial bond with an understanding ally exists to console and inspirit. Though the anguish of wanting to be understood is as heartfelt and poignant as in Jim or Leggatt, what Conrad does now is to use Razumov's profound need for communion as a means of entrapment, of leading the distraught man further into a corrupt life. Of his two hoped-for sympathizers, Prince K—betrays him unwittingly and Mikulin uses him as an instrument of the state. The orphan's need for genuine sympathy is not only unmet but acts insidiously against him. Haldin's doom because of misplaced trust is recapitulated subtly in Razumov's reaching out to misunderstood authority figures. To be sure, Razumov's emotional choice of going to Prince K—predetermines the outcome, supplies wanted confirmation and practical aid. The aristocrat's soft, gray whiskers, with their hint of remembered affection for Razumov, come to suggest sentimentality, effeteness, a pliability to authority that amounts to moral servility. Acceding readily to Mikulin's mystical view that Razumov has been chosen by Providence in this affair, the Prince agrees to help enlist his il-

legitimate son as a spy, reassured by Mikulin's offer of a future career for the patriot. Jim has a Stein, but Conrad denies Razumov a
wise and compassionate elder. No appreciation or sensitivity can be
expected from General T—, who is simply hateful. Antithetical in
temperament and method to his complement Councillor Mikulin, the
general combines fanatic hatred of rebellion with righteous devotion
to work. His haunting goggle eyes (cf. Monygham's nightmares of
Father Beron, his vicious inquisitor) convey concentrated, irrational
force, fixity of purpose, untiring watchfulness, and the dead stare of
a killer. He intimidates and crushes, softening the victim, if he has
not renounced worldly attachments, for the courteous Mikulin, who
induces cooperation and service. Scenting directly the weak points
in Razumov's presentation, General T—presses down just enough to
make Razumov feel netted, exposed by the logic of his own testi-
mony. The general wonders aloud why Haldin should even mention
that he was the assassin "if his object was only to obtain temporary
shelter for a few hours. For, after all, nothing was easier than to say
nothing about it unless, indeed, he were trying, under a crazy misapprehension of your true sentiments, to enlist your assistance—eh,
Mr. Razumov?" (49). And as the interview ends, he advises Razumov
to return home, commenting, "Note that I don't ask Mr. Razumov
whether he has justified his absence to his guest. No doubt he did
this sufficiently. But I don't ask. Mr. Razumov inspires confidence.
It is a great gift" (52). Unerringly suspicious, this guardian of autocracy comprehends that "inspiring confidence" is not to be taken at
face value. "I am his prey—his helpless prey," (49) thinks Razumov,
who, especially in the eyes of the military, is not innocent.

As the shaken Razumov heads back to his rooms, he looks to the
routine and pedestrian for reassurance:

> The exceptional could not prevail against the material contacts which
> make one day resemble another. To-morrow would be like yester-
> day. . . . Extraordinary things do happen. But when they have hap-
> pened they are done with. Thus, too, when the mind is made up. That
> question is done with. And the daily concerns, the familiarities of our
> thought swallow it up—and the life goes on as before with its mys-
> terious and secret sides quite out of sight, as they should be. Life is a
> public thing. (54)

But before a changed moral reality, the surface refuge of normalcy slips away of its own accord. Walled-in again with Haldin, a scene brilliant in its tension and concentrated drama, Razumov is compelled to speak what is tearing at him. A half-veiled confession and justification is guarded and shadowy, but the exposition of his background, political sentiments, and aspirations is a vehement self-definition, a violent throwing off of the responsibility Haldin has imposed on him (and to which he has submitted). The truth of Razumov's separateness pierces Haldin's self-absorption, devastates him with the knowledge that he has unforgivably betrayed the other. "Haldin had a subdued, heartbroken attitude. He bowed his head; his hands hung between his knees. His voice was low and pained but calm. '. . . my action is abhorrent to you. . . . And even my person, too, is loathsome to you perhaps'" (62). An abrupt farewell catches Razumov by surprise. "Haldin, already at the door, tall and straight as an arrow, with his pale face and a hand raised attentively, might have posed for the statue of a daring youth listening to an inner voice" (63). Spontini's "Flight of Youth," imaged forth in this description of Haldin, becomes a metaphor uniting the two students. Having nowhere to go, the certainty and consolation of his martyr's resignation having collapsed, overcome by disillusion and remorse, Haldin as doomed youth anticipates Razumov's futureless self, destined to perpetual flight, without safety, without hope. Both are common victims already trapped. In this regard, compare Marlow's poignant reflection on Jim following the trial: "He was running. Absolutely running, with nowhere to go to. And he was not yet four-and-twenty" (*Lord Jim,* p. 155). In *Under Western Eyes,* this poignancy has darkened to tragic anguish. In contrast, Leggatt disappearing into the blankness of Kohring does not elicit despair. Decoud's nowhere is the Great Isabel.

Haldin's moral drama has a complexity that deepens his humanity and comments on the ambiguities of martyrdom. Haldin's weeping for innocent bomb victims coexists with his continued advocacy of revolutionary violence, less a contradiction than a sign of ideology blunting conscience. But when he understands his great wrong to Razumov, his sense of personal responsibility goes deeper than tears. For the first time he is seized by the intimate consequences of his idealism. In Haldin's flight, one sees him heading not only to his martyr's destiny but also to a self-judged retribution, acquiescing in death because of an afflicted conscience as much as Razumov has

prepared that death for him. Mrs. Haldin intuits that her son seemed
to surrender himself, as if from some unaccountable disheartening.
Martyrdom loses its aura of saintliness, becomes problematic as it is
seen to involve the agonies of doubt and remorse. Cunningly, Mikulin reads to Razumov from the official interrogation record con-
taining the chilling question he composed for the assassin: "Question—Has the man well known to you, in whose rooms you remained
for several hours on Monday and on whose information you have
been arrested—has he had any previous knowledge of your intention to commit a political murder? . . . Prisoner refuses to reply"
(93). It is possible that Haldin, broken by despair, is unable to speak,
but I read his silence as an act of volition and, in particular to Mikulin's question, as a keeping faith with Razumov. Unwilling to take
revenge on his informer, as he might, Haldin partly redeems his injustice to the other, gives to his muteness a dignity beyond revolutionary defiance. In a somewhat similar episode but one lacking dramatic richness, Nostromo on his deathbed scorns to denounce his
adversary Monygham to the waiting communist. Conrad thus gives
Haldin a larger human dimension, granting him a quality of consciousness and moral valor that makes him more than a simple vi-
sionary wedded to ultimate self-sacrifice. Moreover, the exact nature
of Haldin's apparent faltering prior to arrest, like the dismaying fact
of Decoud's suicide, will not enter public knowledge to sully the glow
of enshrinement. Reverence for an idealized portrait is maintained
even while Razumov bears witness to a far different Haldin. Here is
Conrad's sober, ironic tribute to the posthumous power of a man
perceived as a martyr. In firmer command of his art, Conrad achieves
this dual perspective of a famous man without recourse to the protective lie that Marlow offers the Intended or that Emilia uses to
absolve Nostromo.

The political creed Razumov composes after the town clock signals
the hour of Haldin's capture is an ex post facto justification, a clar-
ification and a profession, a means to affirm and formalize his opposition to Haldin:

> History not Theory.
> Patriotism not Internationalism.
> Evolution not Revolution.
> Direction not Destruction.
> Unity not Disruption. (66)

As if to nail down his own doubts, to bury Haldin under a tombstone inscription meant to settle accounts, Razumov stabs his theses over the bed still fresh with Haldin's presence. This deadly, ironic reminder of a crucifix suggests the sacrifice of an ideological foe; thus, Razumov joins his counterpart in having done violence in the name of abstract right. But intellectual formulations cannot still his anxious brooding. In a state of spiritual paralysis, he senses that his avenues to meager happiness, absence of fear and looking forward, have been erased. The thought of being a suspect poisons his every hour, "but the habit of reflection and that desire of safety, of an ordered life, which was so strong in him came to his assistance as the night wore on. His quiet, steady, and laborious existence would vouch at length for his loyalty. There were many permitted ways to serve one's country. There was an activity that made for progress without being revolutionary. The field of influence was great and infinitely varied— once one had conquered a name" (71). But to resume in the old way, to try to suppress the reverberations of what has happened and carry on with a forced indifference, is a cul-de-sac. Guilt drains him of any vestige of self-assurance. The inner structure of his life has crumbled: work ceases to be a haven, detachment is no longer possible.

As outside forces press in, Razumov begins to lose his sense of autonomy. First the gaunt student, member of a radical circle, approaches Razumov with the fact of Haldin's arrest, and this stranger's preconception of Razumov as a mysterious outsider and fellow revolutionist is confirmed by Razumov's unguarded remarks. Furious but apprehensive, Razumov can say nothing to dispel the misguided impression set loose by Haldin's expressions of "warm appreciation" of his character. A vandalistic search of his rooms by the police has its intended effect of disorientation and intimidation. "This disorder affected him profoundly, unreasonably. He sat down and stared. He had a distinct sensation of his very existence being undermined in some mysterious manner, of his moral supports falling away from him one by one" (76–77). Razumov poses an unanswerable question: "I want to guide my conduct by reasonable convictions, but what security have I against something—some destructive horror—walking in upon me as I sit here?" (78). This echo of horror from "Heart of Darkness" is arresting; nature has become politics, both shot through with a menacing, unrelieved, and pervasive uncertainty. Even more uncompromising and bleak in *Under Western*

Eyes than in "Heart of Darkness," Conrad's radical pessimism allows nothing to be trusted, neither in politics nor in the human relations inseparable from it, a prophetic intimation of the totalitarianism of the twentieth century.

This pattern of first one then the other faction contacting Razumov continues with Madcap Kostia, also under the spell of Razumov's putative fame, who offers him money to bolt the police. Kostia's proposal is a comic rendering of Brierly's desperate try to bribe Jim out of sight. The fact that this gesture comes from the festive, spoiled son of an illiterate and wealthy government contractor underlines the pathetic immaturity, the hopeless innocence, of any notion of flight. Jim did run in his own way until he met his destiny in Brown, but Mikulin's unanswerable "Where to?" informs *Under Western Eyes* with an iron law of inescapability, limits, as it were, the novel's geography. In his eagerness to sacrifice for a higher aim and a superior individual, in his simplicity and outlandishness, Kostia calls to mind the Russian harlequin who served Kurtz in the jungle. Conrad's irony is deft. Kostia offers to procure Razumov a getaway disguise, "also a false beard or something of that kind may be needed," and of course his notion of intrigue is incurably theatrical. While Razumov can mock the absurdity of Kostia's misapprehension of him, he also flirts with its possible benefit. "There was an obvious advantage in this conspiracy of mistaken judgment taking him for what he was not. But was it not strange? . . . He had been made a personage without knowing anything about it" (82–83). The process of others fabricating one's identity is subtle in nature and far-reaching in consequence, involving a passivity stemming from an uncertain sense of self. One recalls Marlow allowing his excitable aunt to advance him in a false heroic light, as it turns out a suggestive representation of Kurtz. Likewise, Razumov gains an unmerited fame that allies him with an extremist. In this Kostia exchange, imposture is made explicit, implying the deeper point that Razumov is in disguise from himself. Kostia's suggestion of a costume underscores Razumov's life of counterfeit and comments ironically on his imminent role as secret agent. But for Razumov, both revolutionary hero and patriot of the state are inauthentic selves. And he will masquerade as each, a logical extension of his initial ambivalence toward Haldin and a fate both "deserved" and corrupting.

Primed to face General T—at the other end of a police summons, Razumov is thrown awry by the gentlemanly Mikulin, slight of build, ingratiatingly polite, an exemplar of civility and reasonableness. His mild, diffident manner draws Razumov out (leaving sentences unfinished is particularly effective) at the same time his patient inexpressiveness shakes the informer's tense composure. The beginning of their first interview, breaking off in the text with the councillor's resonating "Where to?", makes clear that Razumov's life is now at the bidding of the authorities. Understandably, Razumov is not ready to comprehend, much less accept, the sickening implications of Mikulin's words. Fearful that he is mistrusted, intent on hiding his complicity, Razumov cannot know that the interrogator is not out to accuse but to get a hold over him, perhaps for some later purpose. Bristling with resistance as Razumov is, Mikulin's demeanor and presentation lay the groundwork for drawing him in. Over time, the official's perfectly attuned approach will make a convert.

The sinister nature of the Mikulin–Razumov relationship makes it a dark reversal of the Marlow–Jim, Captain–Leggatt pairings. Alluding to his university days, confessing a shared predilection for reform, responding to Razumov's detestation of revolutionaries with his own settled opposition to revolt, Mikulin creates over the course of the interview the impression of sympathetic identification, a means to soothe and woo. Undeniably, Mikulin is the only person capable of appreciating Razumov with an intelligence he can respect; essentially, he confirms Razumov in his inauthentic self. But Mikulin's representation of sensitive regard, masterful as performance, is not personal but strategic, its trustworthiness contradicted at face value by his position and the official context of the meeting. Whatever heartening Razumov gains from the man is delusive and short-lived, imparted to make its beneficiary useful, not morally independent. Elsewhere in Conrad, sympathetic understanding, allied to loyalty, is precious and inspiring, the only comfort for the wrongdoer in his desperateness. To Razumov, in need of this attention, the semblance of sympathy is taken for true concern. That Conrad depicts such sympathy here to be manipulative and debasing means that Razumov's ordeal will be the most unrelieved and anguished of Conrad's afflicted heroes, that moral isolation and guilt will be combined at their most intense, that the full burden of inner conflict will be borne by a single consciousness capable of penetrating to truth. The relevant comparisons are with the Congo Marlow, Decoud, and Monygham. Marlow is isolated and suffers prolonged and keen distress, but his complicity in a vile trading operation, and hence sense of guilt, is not as grave, clear-cut, or conscious as Razumov's complicity; furthermore, Marlow is never cowardly, he does not betray a personal appeal for trust or cause another's death; Decoud's agony is ended by suicide; Monygham has the revivifying friendship of Emilia.

Boxed in, Razumov insists repeatedly to Mikulin on his intellectual superiority, as an assertion of self and a line of defense, to contain self-defeating feelings and to present a stance of rightful autonomy, as if mere rationality could hold tyranny at bay. "I know I am but a reed. But I beg you to allow me the superiority of the thinking reed over the unthinking forces that are about to crush him out of existence" (89). "I happen to have been born a Russian with patriotic instincts . . . developed by a faculty of independent thinking—of detached thinking. In that respect I am more free than any social democratic revolution could make me" (98). Razumov frames his antagonism to Haldin on the radical's outrage against reason, the principle with which Razumov identifies himself: "He was a wretch from my point of view, because to keep alive a false idea is a greater crime than to kill a man. . . . I hated him! Visionaries work everlasting evil on earth. Their Utopias inspire in the mass of mediocre minds a disgust of reality and a contempt for the secular logic of human development" (95); "I did not hate him because he had committed the crime of murder. Abhorrence is not hate. I hated him simply because I am sane" (95). In this same tone of the aggrieved party, Razumov protests with disdain the seemingly pointless ransacking of his rooms, delayed for two days. That it was made not merely to jar him, setting the stage for a summons, but also so that Mikulin might sift for clues to the occupant's personality which would afford him advantage in the coming interview, is beyond Razumov's scope of thought.

Overvaluing a strict rationality, not given to suspiciousness, unfamiliar with the subterranean, devious, and base, Razumov is easy game for the subtlety of Mikulin, who is not bound by Razumov's assumption of standards. In his extroversive quality of mind, Razumov is

akin to the young Marlow who navigated the Congo and even to
Decoud, whose intelligence, formidable as it is, could not pierce the
darkness of the Gulf. The philosophy student is rattled by Mikulin's
"dim, unreadable eyes" (95): the inner workings of despotism will not
yield to rational scrutiny. Razumov's thinking belongs to the daylight
world; it implies civilized limits, orderliness, clean-edged lucidity. In
one outburst against police methods, Razumov sounds like an indig-
nant Englishman: "What is all this mockery? Of course, you can send
me straight from this room to Siberia. That would be intelligible. To
what is intelligible I can submit. But I protest against this comedy of
persecution. The whole affair is becoming too comical altogether for
my taste. A comedy of errors, phantoms, and suspicions. It's posi-
tively indecent" (99). Might not Razumov's unpreparedness for political conflict be viewed as an implied warning to Conrad's English
readers, directed against their complacency and exaggerated faith in
norms? Conrad is exposing the insufficiency of reason as well as its
susceptibility to exploitation. To stand a chance of resisting Mikulin's
smooth persuasiveness and other appeals, it is not logic that is needed
but character, not intellectuality but an independent stance, the very
thing Razumov has not forged.[6] And of course by surrendering
Haldin, Razumov has forfeited any autonomy he claims for himself.

Razumov's conception of his own patriotic duty is to wield influence, presumably for gradual liberal reform, once he reaches academic eminence. His five abstract principles ("History not Theory,"
etc.) set him squarely against revolution, which he equates with anarchy. However, the individual course that ensues seems to be quietism, a resigned looking-on while history follows "the secular logic of
human development." Weak because without moral underpinnings,
quietism makes one ripe for victimization as one tends to back off
before encroachment. Retreat for Razumov has been effectively
blocked, signaled by Mikulin's "Where to?" The student cannot defend his attitude of detachment to the councillor because in an autocracy it is indefensible. As Mikulin argues:

> For a man like you . . . such a position is impossible. Don't forget
> that I have seen that interesting piece of paper. I understand your
> liberalism. I have an intellect of that kind myself. Reform for me is
> mainly a question of method. But the principle of revolt is a physical
> intoxication, a sort of hysteria which must be kept away from the masses.

> You agree to this without reserve, don't you? Because, you see, Kirylo
> Sidorovitch, abstention, reserve, in certain situations, come very near
> to political crime. (294)

In truth, Razumov's position is impossible, and to the ominous suggestion that aloofness can be construed as treasonable, Razumov has
no answer. Also unanswerable is Mikulin's reminder of the obligations of patriotism: "You are studying yet, Mr. Razumov, but we are
serving already—don't forget that" (97). Razumov assumes mistak-
enly, out of vanity, unworldliness, a notion of limits, the concentrated need of winning a reputation, perhaps even because of his
very deprivation, that officialdom will honor his privacy, will exempt
him because his scholarly work is responsible and, to him, everything. But Russia is not England.

Mikulin ends their session continuing and reinforcing the note of
flattery and gently modulated pressure, assuring Razumov he will
not be watched, offering his hand in a gesture of friendship and
respect. "Good-bye, Mr. Razumov. An understanding between intelligent men is always a satisfactory occurrence. . . . You are a young
man of great independence. Yes. You are going away free as air, but
you shall end by coming back to us. . . . Some of our greatest minds
had to do that in the end" (295). Then, as if disclosing an innocent
afterthought, Mikulin catches up to a dazed Razumov in the outside
corridor to mention that he may have need of him again. And the
official's parting gambit is brilliant. Responding to the young man's
surprised helplessness, Mikulin plants the idea that Razumov may
have been divinely singled out. "Things are ordered in a wonderful
manner. . . . You have been already the instrument of Providence. . . . Or else what happened to you cannot be accounted for
at all" (296). To a lonely philosophy student with much to brood over,
this suggestion might be expected to be fertile and tantalizing, both
pleasing and subtly corrupting. For Mikulin to put this Russian con-
struction on an extraordinary experience is to impute ever so slightly
to the skeptical Razumov a mysterious and exalted importance, to
hint that salvation lies in bowing to the pressure of destiny (only Mikulin is the prime mover here), is meant finally to erode Razumov's
weakening sense of self-determination. When this notion does surface in Razumov's thoughts amidst his blank wait at home, it is as a
half-hearted try to refute personal responsibility for the complicity

attached to going on Haldin's errand. "'And, after all,' he thought suddenly, 'I might have been the chosen instrument of Providence. This is a manner of speaking, but there may be truth in every manner of speaking. What if that absurd saying were true in its essence?' He meditated for a while, then sat down, his legs stretched out, with stony eyes, and with his arms hanging down on each side of the chair like a man totally abandoned by Providence—desolate" (301). Conrad gives no quarter on this side. From "out there," as if answering Razumov's need if not prayer, will come the summons from Mikulin.

Leaving Mikulin, Razumov retires to the dead end that is his life; the desolation is such that the mind recoils. A defense against the unendurable, Razumov's illness is the last retreat before insanity or suicide. In the nature of a low fever, it "all at once removed him to a great distance from the perplexing actualities, from his very room, even. He never lost consciousness; he only seemed to himself to be existing languidly somewhere very far away from everything that had ever happened to him" (298). The sick man recovers slowly, his eyes opening to an altered moral reality, a dislocation so radical that the confident connection to the everyday and palpable has been severed. "And when he had got back into the middle of things they were all changed, subtly and provokingly in their nature: inanimate objects, human faces, the landlady, the rustic servant-girl, the staircase, the streets, the very air" (298). In a country without justice, anything is possible. With the very idea of normalcy invalidated, no refuge remains, certainly not work. The comfort of his lodgings is the suffocating foretaste of the grave. He clings to this hiding place except to venture out of habit to the University, and "it followed that whenever he went abroad he felt himself at once closely involved in the moral consequences of his act. It was there that the dark prestige of the Haldin mystery fell on him, clung to him like a poisoned robe it was impossible to fling off" (299). The terrible thought obtrudes: "Was it possible that he no longer belonged to himself?" (301). Despite the austerity of his life, Razumov is no stoic. After three weeks of solitary torment pass without word from Mikulin, he collapses utterly. "Everything abandoned him—hope, courage, belief in himself, trust in men. His heart had, as it were, suddenly emptied itself. It was no use struggling on. Rest, work, solitude, and the frankness of intercourse with his kind were alike forbidden to him. Everything was gone. His existence was a great cold blank" (303).

Depleted and will-less, Razumov is now ready to clasp the extended hand of the councillor. The summons arrives. Not to overstate Mikulin's importance or power, Conrad sketches in the man's later downfall as a further indictment of Russian autocracy, to whom all are expendable, all are potential victims. But now, to Mikulin's good fortune and ostensibly Razumov's, this "civilian of superior rank" is promoted to direct police supervision over Europe. (This element of chance in society is the correlate to the accident found in Conrad's natural world.) If not for the advancement, Mikulin would have had no immediate use for Razumov, who would have remained adrift, wasting away from dry rot. With a certain eagerness, Razumov goes to this and several other contacts, but he does not enlist merely as flight from despair. Firmer cause is needed for an agent's reliability. "The obscure, unrelated young student Razumov, in the moment of great moral loneliness, was allowed to feel that he was an object of interest to a small group of people of high position" (307–8). This show of concern from a select circle answers Razumov's need for distinction, appeals to his sense of ambition and self-importance. Thus, Razumov is snared by his own aspirations, collaborates in his own seduction. "And there was some pressure, too, besides the persuasiveness. Mr. Razumov was always being made to feel that he had committed himself" (308), as indeed he had. And in Mikulin's presence, Razumov's guilt over Haldin is mitigated. Their clandestine meetings use the cover of an oculist's office, and in a novel about seeing, Conrad may be entering too readily into Razumov's mockingly contemptuous spirit, showing how easy it is to pull the wool over the eyes of revolutionaries. When a student radical comes with a warning of imminent arrest, the green shade over Razumov's eye serves as simple expedient to explain his medical visits, and none too subtly it implies Razumov's moral obtuseness, his impaired understanding of the meaning and consequences of a duplicitous existence. Giving permission for the artless Kostia to filch money from his father for which he, Razumov, has no use is mere play, hardly an impressive exercise in malice or ideological hatred. Kostia's obedience is amazing to Razumov because his masquerade is taken seriously, is proceeding with its own momentum. Eager loyalty incarnate, Kostia insists on driving Razumov by sledge out of the city, and this little melodrama of flight is an ironic version of Haldin's escape plan. In taking the sleigh ride that was to have been his adversary's, in stepping into the role Haldin has prepared unintentionally for him, Razumov submits to a subtle process whereby, in unforeseen ways, he begins to become increasingly knit to the dead youth. (Compare Marlow stepping into the shoes of his predecessor Captain Fresleven, speared to death by a Congo native. Both Marlow and Razumov endure an unearned identity which becomes gradually more noxious.) The creation of Haldin, the carrier of Haldin's memory to the exiled Russians, the living vestige of a son and brother to Haldin's family, Razumov is slipping deeper into the other's skin.

III

BY WITHHOLDING until late into the Geneva section the clinching evidence via flashback to corroborate our suspicions that Razumov is an agent, Conrad directs us to weigh inner reasons to account for his appearance in Switzerland. Guerard suggests as plausible speculations "a self-destructive tempting of fate; a compulsion to confront those most likely to destroy him; even, an unconscious effort to appease guilt through reenactment of the crime."[7] I would include also the desire for revenge, for with Haldin safely dead and Razumov's own murderous anger unmitigated, only the martyr's compatriots can be objects for retaliation. Furthermore, Conrad's technique of delaying the factual revelation preserves reader sympathy for Razumov as we witness his keen distress and understand the odiousness of his sham life.[8] His suffering comes to us undiluted by the sure knowledge of his police status and reminds us, regardless of any undercover work, of the real danger he faces. By deemphasizing Razumov as spy, Conrad has largely succeeded in neutralizing the unsavoriness attached to him for being a government informer. Even when his official role is verified, our conception of him scarcely alters because Conrad dramatizes him with such vividness and completeness, because Razumov is unable to maintain a barrier of cool distance from his contacts, and because we are made to think of him primarily as Haldin's betrayer. We remember also that he does not serve as a volunteer or with wholehearted conviction, that he is not solaced by the promise of material reward. The contents of the only police report he writes are kept from us, and we do not know how damaging, if at all, this information is against the conspirators. Thus, Razumov's conflict remains intensely personal, and the fact that he is Mikulin's agent is subordinated to the gripping drama of conscience. Razumov's prevailing tone of bitterness and sarcasm betrays the corrosiveness of guilt. At the same time, it is the only means of relief, barring a full confession, from an intolerable position. Imposture is made more detestable to Razumov by his having to accept the hateful persona of revolutionary hero, as Haldin's accomplice to be indebted ironically to his nemesis. Razumov's bitterness flows also from a clenched rage at his ruined life, destroyed by these people whom he disdains and whose trust he must court. And his intellectual pride, beleaguered and insulted, threatens to sabotage his disguise.

The fierce ironies built into Razumov's situation are part of the force of opposition Conrad enlists trying to break his protagonist's self-sufficiency. Even as Razumov sneers at the radicals, Conrad tests and punishes him, probing for weaknesses and needling him for his pride, in an effort to make him worthy of the doomed heroism to come. The sheer contempt Razumov feels for Peter, the humiliation of being embraced by this hoary feminist, praised and brought into his confidence, cannot be suppressed. Identifying Peter as the center of revolutionary action which drew him to Geneva, Razumov ostensibly flatters but secretly ridicules his celebrated interlocutor: "What else has drawn me near you, do you think? It is not what all the world knows of you surely. It's precisely what the world at large does not know. I was irresistibly drawn—let us say impelled, yes, impelled; or, rather, compelled, driven—driven" (227). Razumov pursues this vein "with a satanic enjoyment of the scorn prompting him to play with the greatness of the great man—'Ah, Peter Ivanovitch, if you only knew the force which drew—no, which *drove* me towards you! The irresistible force'" (228). Repulsed by having to lie directly and answering to inward necessities, Razumov spits out a mock confession which is also the desperate voice of individuality. "You must render me the justice that I have not tried to please. I have been impelled, compelled, or rather sent—let us say sent—towards you for a work that no one but myself can do. . . . Here I stand before you—confessed! But one thing more I must add to complete it: a mere blind tool I can never consent to be" (228–29). In the midst of deriding this archpriest of revolution, Conrad can still turn his esteemed phrase of moral solidarity from *Lord Jim* against Razumov, and put into Peter's mouth the irony becomes more stinging. "You are one of us—*un des nôtres*" (210), exclaims Peter to the famous newcomer. Conrad's savage portrait of Madame de S—is conveyed in descriptive imagery of death and rigidity, and if nothing is to be feared from this painted spiritualist, Conrad, nevertheless, uses the interview with her to keep the pressure on Razumov. Peter's effusions on her intuitive gifts seem to taunt Razumov, who once yearned desperately to be understood. Her blank, lifeless eyes jar him with the memory of Mikulin's unnerving stares. When Razumov drops into French to assure Madame that his reserve is a respectful way of listening, she nods approval to Peter and murmurs, "Later on in the diplomatic service." "The fantastic absurdity of it revolted him because it seemed to outrage his ruined hopes with the vision of a mock-career" (220).

Razumov recognizes his real adversary in Sophia, valued by Conrad for her veteran's toughness and personal moral code, a descendant of the French lieutenant in *Lord Jim*. "Stripped of rhetoric, mysticism, and theories, she was the true spirit of destructive revolution" (261). The wrongheadedness Conrad attributes to her in his Author's Note, a mild reproof if applied to her activism, is demonstrated only in her unqualified regard for Peter. Dialogue between Razumov and Sophia is lively, keen, and balanced. Having gathered from a comrade's letter that Razumov attended lectures on the morning of the assassination and did not seek to escape afterward, Sophia pays a professional's tribute to his courage. "I call such coolness superb—that's all. It is proof of uncommon strength of character" (255), an assessment which foreshadows her informed judgment at the novel's end. But now this undeserved praise has no effect on Razumov's self-respect. In an almost casual recounting of his actions on the crucial day, especially plausible to the earnest Sophia because understated and indicative of fortitude, Razumov toys with the truth in manufacturing a version to satisfy her curiosity. At one point, as if in brazen, spiteful play, he becomes Haldin slipping undetected into his own lodgings. No one saw him return, he tells her. "I went up like a shadow. It was a murky morning. The stairs were dark. I glided up like a phantom. Fate? Luck?" (257). As Conrad implies in their exchanges, soldierly virtues are no match for the deviousness of the intriguer. Warily attentive as Sophia builds a theory of treachery and justice around Ziemianitch from information supplied in her St. Petersburg letter, Razumov must relive mentally his incriminating episode with the peasant, the one weakness in his otherwise perfect credentials. Razumov succeeds in giving Sophia confidence in her reconstructed account of what happened to Haldin, so close to the facts yet brilliantly to his advantage, surviving this last danger of exposure and even enjoying the teasing disparity between the woman's inferences and his privileged knowledge. Ziemianitch's suicide seems like Providence's gift in erasing all doubt as to Haldin's betrayer. Sophia's linking the wrongdoer with the devil does not dismay Razumov but occasions a triumphant satisfaction, feeds his superiority, persuades him that he is above the remorse Sophia ascribes to the suicide. Indeed, Razumov has withstood the workings of conventional conscience and thereby cut himself loose from the invisible restraints of community. If God is of no account, this freedom can lead to partnership with the devil. It is as if Conrad has discovered that his moral structures are formulas, that something more intimate and searing is wanted to pierce his would-be Kurtz with recognition. Conditioned to a lifetime of loneliness and justified in his own eyes, Razumov emerges from these duels, as he claims, "a match for them all" (254).

Razumov must bear simultaneously the considerable psychological pressure Conrad exerts, and while no one aspect of his ordeal buckles him, the cumulative price of his encounters is high. During an interview with Peter, acute anxiety and revulsion prompt him to imagine knifing the man and fleeing, but he arrests this underside of himself and fears suddenly for his sanity. The strain of his dual existence threatens dissociation. After leaving the loathsome pair in the Château Borel, "he felt, bizarre as it may seem, as though another self, an independent sharer of his mind, had been able to view his whole person very distinctly indeed. . . . 'How am I to go on day after day if I have no more power of resistance—moral resistance'" (230)? To be incessantly vigilant drains the will. In sharp dialogue with Sophia, he "noted the slightest shades in this conversation, which he had not expected, for which he was not prepared.

That was it. 'I was not prepared,' he said to himself. 'It has taken me unawares.' It seemed to him that if he only could allow himself to pant openly like a dog for a time this oppression would pass away. 'I shall never be found prepared,' he thought, with despair" (252). Hating that "degrading method of direct lying which at times he found it almost impossible to practice" (279–80) can only exacerbate self-contempt; and by living a lie, bound to the tyranny of a fictitious identity, he must war constantly against his spontaneity. Facing Nikita's squeaking envy and suspicions, "he made a gesture of despair. It was not his courage that failed him. The choking fumes of falsehood had taken him by the throat—the thought of being condemned to struggle on and on in that tainted atmosphere without the hope of ever renewing his strength by a breath of fresh air" (269). Despite all, he does not crack, and something far more powerful and unlooked-for must grip him before he can own up to the truth. Much earlier, disconsolate in his St. Petersburg lodgings, he had said angrily to himself: "If one only could go and spit it all out at some of them—and take the consequences" (302). The novel is building steadily for that climactic moment.

Events conspire to bring Razumov an unforeseen guarantee of security. "No more need of lies. I shall have only to listen and to keep my scorn from getting the upper hand of my caution" (284). Ironically, Conrad grants Razumov the safety he had long cherished both to expose its illusoriness and to establish the conditions for self-confrontation. The apparent confirmation of Razumov's trustworthiness recalls the opportunity Conrad offers Nostromo to purloin the silver everyone believes to have sunk. With suspicion removed, perfect safety makes possible the perfect crime, where the only threat is oneself. As we learn from his diary entries, Razumov was contemplating "the unpardonable sin" of stealing Natalie's soul. His retreat to Rousseau's Island, where he writes a police report before beginning his journal, is akin to the captain in "The Secret Sharer" retiring to his cabin in signaling a turning inward, an introspection that precedes receptivity and self-mastery. But Razumov's dubious safety has been purchased at the cost of further detachment, and geographical separation signifies his untouchable loneliness. Embedded in the pejorative description of the islet is Conrad's contempt for Geneva and its inhabitants. "There was something of naïve, odious, and inane simplicity about the unfrequented tiny crumb of earth named after Jean Jacques Rousseau. Something pretentious and shabby, too" (290). The "pretentious and shabby" might apply to the gesture of a city which could condemn its son and, once he had achieved fame, commemorate him posthumously with a token park, one removed from the mainland as if from fear of taint. A fitting soul mate for Razumov, Rousseau was an outsider, exile, and vagabond, suffered a wretched childhood, felt persecuted throughout his life, and harbored strong guilt feelings. That Razumov's diary is begun under the shadow of the man who authored *Confessions* suggests on one level that *Under Western Eyes* may be read as Conrad's spiritual autobiography. And might not Razumov composing in this solitude serve as an image of Conrad the novelist?

Back in the city, Razumov soon visits the Haldins, ostensibly to solidify his gain. Not to report Sophia's information might put him in a bad light. However, he receives no satisfaction in repeating Sophia's grim tale to the mother, another victim of her son's recklessness.

> The fifteen minutes with Mrs. Haldin were like the revenge of the unknown: that white face, that weak, distinct voice; that head, at first turned to him eagerly, then, after a while, bowed again and motionless . . . had troubled him like some strange discovery. And there seemed to be a secret obstinacy in that sorrow, something he had not expected. Was it hostile? But it did not matter. Nothing could touch him now; in the eyes of the revolutionaries there was now no shadow on his past. (340)

Certainly, no pious fraud, even if Razumov were so disposed, could assuage her woe. Another sign of the deromanticized nature of this novel is the absence of any charitable lie involving a woman. Marlow's chivalrous untruth to the Intended and Emilia's falsehood shielding Nostromo hinted at Conrad's turning aside from the darkest implications of his vision. In *Under Western Eyes*, Conrad spares neither his characters nor himself. For Mrs. Haldin, there is only "suffering without remedy" (339). Petrified in time, she sorrows for the head that will never rest in her lap. Razumov chooses to ignore any rebuke implied by her terrible silence, an unanswerable challenge to his own grievances. Nevertheless, her bereavement touches his buried humanity, pity stirs beneath his severity and anger. For the first time, he feels compassion for another's pain. Implicit, but beyond his reach, is the truth that his personal ruin is not to be laid exclusively on Victor Haldin but is ultimately the tragedy of his country, of history. Multitudes of lives have been struck, the mother epitomizing perhaps the sorrow of a nation, an image of eternal mourning. But Razumov's feelings of outrage are too intense for sustained empathy. "He had felt a pitying surprise. But that, of course, was of no importance. Mothers did not matter. He could not shake off the poignant impression of that silent, quiet, white-haired woman, but a sort of sternness crept into his thoughts. These were the consequences. Well, what of it? 'Am I then on a bed of roses' " (340)? The woman's prolonged muteness, with her rigid pose as if in infinite disappointment, inflames his old anger against Haldin. Regardless of Razumov's direct knowledge, Haldin's reputation cannot be altered by anything he might say. Thus, Razumov becomes Haldin's "victim" a second time, having to concede the omnipotence of his saintly memory. Contemplating the mother, he realizes no one will mourn for him, for his broken life, yet everyone remembers the other. Razumov's own claims cannot defeat Haldin's spiritual essence.[9]

> And was it not something like enviousness which gripped his heart, as if of a privilege denied to him alone of all the men that had ever passed through this world? It was the other who had attained to repose and yet continued to exist in the affection of that mourning old woman, in the thoughts of all these people posing for lovers of humanity. It was impossible to get rid of him. 'It's myself whom I have given up to destruction,' thought Razumov. 'He has induced me to do it. I can't shake him off.' (341)

Stunned by these recognitions, Haldin's invincibility (he is named aptly Victor) and the self-destructiveness implicit in the betrayal, Razumov flees from the room only to encounter Natalie. Indeed, Haldin is everywhere. "Her presence in the ante-room was as unforeseen as the apparition of her brother had been" (341). Natalie incarnates Victor's living spirit. Conrad has plotted deftly for this identification to prepare for the two confessions, which are inspired by the agency of Haldin's soul and mark Razumov's assumption of freedom.

Haldin's legacy is to shape the destinies of Natalie and Razumov, leading to their mature independence. Conrad has already established a marked kinship between Haldin and Razumov that develops through the novel: in various ways the students are victims of czarism; both have a callowness and a critical blindness in grasping consequences; each misapprehends with disastrous results the true nature of his confidant; both are driven by desperation and resort to mysticism before committing an irresponsible act. Even more than the hate and anger, remorse grafts Razumov to his victim, and their inseparability is reinforced by Razumov's life of masquerade. As Haldin's appendage and bogus creation, Razumov conspires in the debasement of his own soul. Muffled, he becomes increasingly the victim of impersonation, falling more and more under Haldin's spell. When his heart is touched by being brought into the family, when need for Natalie strips away his scorn, he comes to feel most intimately the burden of being Haldin's surrogate. Conrad has prepared us carefully to think of Razumov as Haldin's replacement. Natalie tells the professor that she does not equate Victor's absence with death. "But lost people do turn up even in Russia. Do you know what my last hope is? Perhaps the next thing we know, we shall see him walking into our rooms" (110). Her words recall Haldin's materialization in Razumov's chambers, and of course Razumov's appearance in Geneva is unforeseen, as if Natalie has evoked him. Sibling affection will be transferred to the brother's comrade and determine her growing love for him. The professor is quite explicit with the newcomer when he discusses the effect of Victor's loss on Natalie: "The very groundwork of active existence for Natalie Haldin is gone with him. Can you wonder then that she turns with eagerness to the only man her brother mentions in his letters. Your name is a sort of legacy" (190). When Natalie entrusts Razumov with the responsibility for comforting her mother, imposing on him an awesome obligation much as her brother did, she appeals to him as if he were Haldin's successor: "I don't want to abuse your sympathy, but you must understand that it is in you that we can find all that is left of his generous soul" (346). The namelessness Razumov discloses to Peter refers factually to his absence of family, but more importantly it suggests an identity as yet unprofessed, a lack of authenticity in the double sense of imposture and unsureness of self: "I have no name. . . . The very patronymic you are so civil as to use when addressing me I have no legal right to—but what of that? I don't wish to claim it. I have no father" (208). As the dynamics of Razumov's conflict evolve, Haldin will become Razumov's spiritual father, bequeathing to him an "I" that must be both honored and repudiated. Haldin's spiritual inheritance extends also to Natalie, who embodies the purest and best part of her brother, his faith in humanity and the future, his generosity of heart, forgiveness, and selfless devotion to Russia. However, as a figure of reconciliation, she does not league herself with terrorism, and thus Conrad distinguishes her from Peter's group. In her simple black dress and sheltered upbringing, she resembles Emilia and her cloistered youth. Eager for guidance, Natalie is moved to follow her brother. "All the significance of freedom, its indefinite promises, lived in their long discussions, which breathed the loftiest hope of action and faith in success. . . . What she wanted was to learn almost at any cost how she could remain faithful to his departed spirit" (140). She carries the idealized misconception of Razumov implanted in her by Victor, is attracted similarly by Razumov's mysterious reserve, and likewise forces an unwanted confidence on him. Hence, Natalie duplicates symbolically and powerfully her brother's charged episode with Razumov.

Escaping from Mrs. Haldin, Razumov comes face to face with Natalie, perceived as a glowing reminder of Victor. As he notes later in his diary: "The most trustful eyes in the world—your brother said of you when he was as well as a dead man already. And when you stood before me with your hand extended, I remembered the very sound of his voice, and I looked into your eyes—and that was enough. I knew that something had happened, but I did not know then what" (358). With Victor, Razumov had acquiesced in his confidence, submitted to a charge despite feelings which belied the impression of sympathy, and violated the pledge thus established. The conditions of this primal situation are recreated with Victor's heir, and Razumov is on the verge of a second betrayal, stealing Natalie's soul. But here the vicious cycle ends. Lovely Natalie inspires Razumov to become his best self, loosens the crust of bitterness over his heart. As he writes to her in his journal:

> You were appointed to undo the evil by making me betray myself back into truth and peace. You! And you have done it in the same way, too, in which he ruined me: by forcing upon me your confidence. . . . Victor Haldin had stolen the truth of my life from me, who had nothing else in the world, and he boasted of living on through you on this earth where I had no place to lay my head. (358–59)

> I felt that I must tell you that I had ended by loving you. And to tell you that I must first confess. Confess, go out—and perish.

> Suddenly you stood before me! You alone in all the world to whom
> I must confess. You fascinated me—you have freed me from the
> blindness of anger and hate—the truth shining in you drew the truth
> out of me. (361)

Before the horrified girl, Razumov presses a denunciatory finger,
like a pistol barrel, to his breast, and this image of violence against
the self prefigures the self-inflicted wound of Razumov's deafening,
self-inflicted in the sense that he chooses to confess before Haldin's
compatriots expecting savage retribution. When Nikita strikes with
open hand over his victim's ear, Razumov "heard a faint, dull det-
onating sound, as if someone had fired a pistol on the other side of
the wall" (368–69). The frequency and dramatic power of suicide in
Conrad's opus has been noted often and derives no doubt from his
attempted suicide at twenty by shooting himself in the chest.[10] However, Razumov's apparently suicidal public confession is convincing
in its own right. Though Razumov's survival is all-important, the
metaphor of a gunshot associated with his deafening echoes with the
actual shots which kill Jim and Decoud. Doramin slays Jim, who ap-
proached execution voluntarily, with one bullet flush in the heart,
and Decoud ends his life with a pistol shot through the chest. Nostromo's death, like Heyst's self-immolation, is melodramatic and forced,
which prompts exclusion from this grouping. Razumov does not betray again, and thus symbolically he undoes the original deed, gives
proof of moral growth. This time he refuses to take advantage of a
Haldin's defenselessness. Confession kills the loving image Natalie
has of Razumov, and this wrenching disillusionment has the effect
of saving her from being drawn in by Peter. Thus, Razumov's act
has a redeeming quality in helping to launch her independence.

Fierce antipathy toward Haldin seems to have constituted the driving force, the intimate justification, for Razumov to have continued
as he was. Because of mother and daughter, he realizes that his vicious feelings are both futile and corruptive. Razumov's remorse fo-
cuses on the evil he has brought on himself, but remorse for Haldin's
sake, an acknowledgment that informing was also a violation against
the other, is implicit in his second confession; essentially, he is giving
his life in payment for Haldin's. But while Razumov is conscience-
striken, evident in his embrace of truth and willingness to accept consequences (loss of Natalie's love, the end of any career in Russia, the

revolutionaries' ire), he is not contrite. One might expect that the remorse which precedes confession would involve shaken self-esteem, a humbling, an implicit appeal for forgiveness. Prior to the initial confession, in response to Razumov's leading questions about Ziemianitch, Natalie had dissociated herself from the duty of revenge, and this mercy to the alleged betrayer gives Razumov some comfort. Emilia, Natalie's obvious forebear, heard Nostromo's deathbed confession and forgave him. But the only softening Razumov feels is a stab of pity for Mrs. Haldin and need for Natalie. It is true that now he admits to a conventional conscience, that his pride is informed by a sense of resignation, that he has been touched by love, which, however brief and foredoomed, has saved him from forsaking his humanity altogether. But no self-abasement is evident in either of his confessions. By asserting the truth, Razumov throws off the suffocating yoke of a fabricated identity, breaks free of duplicity, separates from Haldin, and becomes himself. Subsequent diary entries to Natalie give proof of his new strength and clarity: "I, too, had my guiding idea; and remember that, amongst us, it is more difficult to lead a life of toil and self-denial than to go out in the street and kill from conviction" (358). And: "In giving Victor Haldin up, it was myself, after all, whom I have betrayed most basely. . . . Only don't be deceived, Natalia Victorovna, I am not converted. Have I then the soul of a slave? No! I am independent— and therefore perdition is my lot" (361–62).

Razumov's second confession causes two serious objections. Karl regards it as a novelistic flaw and Howe sees it as proceeding from Conrad's political hatreds. Since Razumov holds the revolutionaries in such contempt, why then does he suppose them worthy to hear his confession, Howe asks. He considers this scene "a critical instance of the way bias run wild can damage a political novel. By refusing to extend to his radicals the necessary credit, if only later to call it in, Conrad fails to establish the dramatic ground for his denouement."[11] But in this instance the worthiness of Razumov's listeners is hardly the point. It is a measure of the forces driving Razumov that he displays neither hesitancy nor any sense of compromise in exposing himself before perceived inferiors. Surely, Conrad is doing justice to the urgency of guilt compelling raw confession and to the simultaneous need for punishment that will appease guilt. Karl, on

134 Joseph Conrad: Consciousness and Integrity

the other hand, finds the weakness stemming from Conrad's failure to establish a proper climax. "If Razumov's confession to Miss Haldin and *not* to the revolutionaries is seen as the dramatic climax, then all the later business at Laspara's house becomes superfluous. It is Miss Haldin who causes Razumov's confession; his love for her and not his feelings of guilt toward the revolutionaries leads to inner conflict."[12] But rather than anticlimactic, this repeated confession is an extension of the climax, a psychological playing-out of guilt and an imperative assertion of autonomy. Confession to Natalie alone is insufficient, and Razumov notes in his diary the necessity of having to face the extremists: "I suffer horribly, but I am not in despair. There is only one more thing to do for me. After that—if they let me—I shall go away and bury myself in obscure misery" (361). Resigned to an inglorious future if permitted, Razumov does not seek to escape by suicide in proclaiming himself to his enemies, however perilous that disclosure. Aside from the diminution of self, not to face the consequences now would leave him forever a marked man. To remain as he is in Geneva is to court retaliation. An exposed agent is no longer serviceable, and he cannot retreat from his earned independence to petition Mikulin for aid. To return to academic studies is unthinkable, and exile elsewhere was never a viable alternative. Any "vanishing," like Jim to Patusan or like Leggatt, would leave the issue incomplete, create an impression of cowardice, keep the guilt virulent. Disappearance is a romantic expedient, a flight from conscience, which Conrad knows to be damaging and illusory. Haldin had requested of Razumov, "All I want you to do is to help me to vanish" (20). *Under Western Eyes* is not the work for hopeful second chances. Shift the emphasis of that second confession away from authorial prejudice or artistic miscalculation to Razumov's psychology and his conduct becomes not just credible but essential. Furthermore, this public revelation is an expression of Razumov's principled opposition to revolution. The courage he displays now is not merely compelled by guilt but rests on his political convictions and belief in his own independence. Indeed, his last words before he is assaulted from behind proclaim him a free man:

> I beg you to observe . . . that I had only to hold my tongue. To-day, of all days since I came amongst you, I was made safe, and to-day I made myself free from falsehood, from remorse—independent of every single human being on this earth. (368)

By having the sadistic double agent Nikita commit the unauthorized outrage, which intensifies its sordidness, Conrad refrains from needlessly vilifying his revolutionaries. Conrad distinguishes further the personally moral from the ideological by having Sophia "off-stage" (she has already left for Russia), thus divorcing her from the act, which she repudiates expressly in the novel's concluding pages. The extremity of Razumov's physical suffering (I include also his mutilation by the streetcar) reflects the enormity of Razumov's transgression in Conrad's eyes as well as a fully realized conception of integrity.

The resistances and uncertainties felt in Conrad's portrayal of Jim's death are entirely absent in the treatment of Razumov's final accounting, where Conrad has achieved a finer justice and a higher level of art. Jim's irresponsible release of Brown repeats his *Patna* failure in leadership with fatal consequences, whereas Razumov does not betray again, indicative of significant change. An element of self-glorification colors Jim's acceptance of execution before mostly loving and grief-stricken followers, which diminishes the stature Conrad is reaching for with his romantic, but no suggestion of heroics clouds the moral nature of Razumov's confession before an utterly hostile gathering. Jim's proud, tight-lipped silence contrasts pointedly with Razumov's self-possessed articulation. A father surrogate does not administer the necessary penalty, breaking a pattern evident in Lingard, Doramin, and Viola as agents of justice punishing their betraying adopted sons Willems, Jim, and Nostromo, respectively, who all die in exile. Jim's punishment is clean, swift, and dignified, suggesting authorial protectiveness; Conrad is uninhibited in imagining Razumov's brutalization and trolley accident, during which the victim loses consciousness only after making known his deafness to those who carry his smashed body to the sidewalk. Razumov's independence from remorse, the debt owed to the past, seems to be Conrad's own, which permits at last a worthy return to the homeland. Jim passes into legend, but Razumov is restored to his country, nursed by Tekla and clinging to life, a man speaking.

With several deft touches, Conrad persuades us of the absolute rightness of Tekla's union with Razumov. In conversation with Natalie, Tekla explains her leaving home as an effort to make herself useful to "the utterly hopeless. . . . I mean the people who have nowhere to go and nothing to look forward to in this life. Do you understand how frightful that is—nothing to look forward to" (150)! Her aspiration is linked with Razumov's plight, the verbal echo alluding to his despairing realization in St. Petersburg that as General T—'s suspect, he no longer has possibilities for happiness. And of course the futurelessness of both will be alleviated in a purposeful life together after Geneva. The helpless lithographer Andrei, whom she tends for several months, a political victim tortured into a false confession incriminating others (cf. Monygham), is the first object of her calling. His broken body, imminent death, and act of betrayal make him a precursor of Razumov, who will become her true charge. That her first patient died wretchedly, crushed by remorse, is Conrad's reminder of the devastation exacted by unappeased guilt. Lonely and nameless, Tekla and Razumov are meant for each other. As she says to him during their initial meeting: "No one is told my name. No one cares. No one talks to me, no one writes to me. My parents don't even know if I'm alive. I have no use for a name, and I have almost forgotten it myself" (235). Tekla will assume Razumov's name in chaste marriage, as she will be brought to life by his total reliance on her. While Tekla is unfit for independent life because temperamentally she must serve and because deserting Peter outright is dangerous, Razumov attains his destined independence at the cost of worldly existence. Conrad rewards her "starving, grotesque, and pathetic devotion" (234) with a courteous and worthy partner, at the same time showing compassion to Razumov, who has never known a woman's succoring affection. Razumov replaces Peter for her, another noted talker honored by visitors. In offering to be of use to Razumov, Tekla had complained, "What's the good of speech to me? Who would ever want to hear what I could say" (237)? In their alliance, Razumov speaks for her, and his voice is her achievement also in that she nurses his shattered body. Now her help is appreciated and effective, whereas her ministrations to the guilt-plagued Andrei could not reach him and Peter's cruelty to her and gross self-absorption made him untouchable.

Conrad infuses their union with his rare tenderness and a symbolic familial character as Razumov's subtle merging with Victor is balanced by the establishment of Tekla as a double of Mrs. Haldin. By being disregarded in the Château Borel, not listened to, Tekla has been reduced to the equivalent of speechlessness. After Razumov's fifteen minutes with Mrs. Haldin, she lapses into a terrible silence born of mistrust. Of the people who matter, only she does not respond to Razumov with confidence. Disbelieving him, she "had nothing to say to any one—not even to her daughter" (372). The diminished importance Tekla gives to her words, which seems too patly to complement Razumov's deafness, may have a deeper meaning in connection with Mrs. Haldin's silence. For Razumov to have lost his hearing suggests that accusing voices, internal and otherwise, perhaps the most feared being the mother's, have been stilled. In this sense deafness is a reconciliation with conscience, an achieved inner peace. Tekla's "speechlessness," her depreciation of her own speech, neutralizes the mother's accusatory silence. Mrs. Haldin forever waiting to regain her son's head in her lap is transformed into Tekla comforting Razumov on the streetcar, fulfilled in her expectancy, unconditional in her embrace. Razumov becomes the son to Tekla the mother, a "relation," she informs the trolley passengers as she claims him on the ride to the hospital. "She sat down calmly, and took his head on her lap" (371). Perhaps here, implied in Tekla's cradling solicitude, is the forgiveness the true mother Mrs. Haldin could never grant and for which Razumov could never ask.

Expressions of nonviolent service knit the "orphans" Tekla, Razumov, and Natalie, a value which emerges as part of the novel's muted affirmation. The two women are associated more closely as Tekla represents a possible fate for the girl; her shabbiness, worn-out youth, unappreciated labors stand as a warning of what might befall Natalie should she come under Peter's sway. In addition, Tekla's disenchantment with a great figure anticipates Natalie's own disillusionment with a man overvalued by virtue of reputation. Maturation through radical loss enables Natalie, like Tekla, to discover her life's work. When the professor visits after Mrs. Haldin's funeral, he responds to Natalie's striking composure, a description which evokes the captain's appreciation of Leggatt:

> With her arms folded she walked up and down the whole length of the room, talking slowly, smooth-browed, with a resolute profile. She gave me a new view of herself, and I marvelled at that something grave and measured in her voice, in her movements, in her manner. It was the perfection of collected independence. The strength of her nature had come to surface because the obscure depths had been stirred. (373)

Her fullness of being rests on self-abnegation. "There was no longer any Natalie Haldin, because she had completely ceased to think of herself. It was a great victory, a characteristically Russian exploit in self-suppression" (375).

As a way of life, the intimate sphere fails invariably for Conrad's people; collective effort may satisfy their yearnings for purpose. Private tragedy leading to patriotic endeavor is underscored in "Prince Roman," where the nobleman transcends bereavement over his young wife's death and joins Poland's 1830–31 uprising against the Russian oppressor. "Her loss had been to him a moral shock. It had opened his heart to a greater sorrow, his mind to a vaster thought, his eyes to all the past and to the existence of another love fraught with pain but as mysteriously imperative as that lost one to which he had entrusted his happiness" (*Tales of Hearsay*, p. 41). Thereafter, through a lifetime of suffering and devoted activity, the prince attains the highest renown. With Natalie's loss of family and idealistic personal love, the same love which dooms Emilia to sorrow, she goes to pursue humanitarian work in Russia. Mrs. Gould will continue to aid the community albeit with a sad devotion, shackled by a hollow marriage, rank, and foreign sensibility. However, Natalie has no such constraints. Reared in a political atmosphere, unattached, close in spirit to her people, she retains an inspired vision. Despite all, her voice remains hopeful and stirring, a counterpoint, one assumes, to the substance and tone of Razumov's speech. I imagine Razumov with an attitude of tragic resignation about which Conrad wrote admiringly elsewhere. "Resignation, not mystic, not detached, but resignation open-eyed, conscious, and informed by love, is the only one of our feelings for which it is impossible to become a sham" (A Familiar Preface to *A Personal Record*, p. xix). In the course of explaining himself, Victor had remarked to Razumov, "Men like me leave no posterity" (22), an observation that Conrad has General T—repeat, "That brood leaves no posterity" (51). But Victor does engender spiritual progeny, for through their connection with him, Natalie and Razumov come to express a selfless patriotism (whose spirit animated Victor, however misguided his practice), each at the same time and in a distinct way apart from him. The sister of course disavows violence and turns away from Peter's circle. Haldin's legacy to Razumov has been to mature his soul through suffering, to transmute him into a voice. (As a result of his life and death closeness with Kurtz, Marlow is indebted to the other for moral identity and grows into a contemplative voice.) Aside from purely personal reasons, including a hunger for fame, Razumov had envisaged academic distinction as a means of serving his country. And in the intellectual authority Razumov has acquired through conflict, purged now of selfishness, Conrad's understated irony suggests that he has won a deserved stature. The fact that Sophia visits him in the south of Russia surprises the narrowly judgmental professor, but her discriminating praise substantiates Conrad's approval: "Some of *us* always go to see him when passing through. He is intelligent. He has ideas. . . . He talks well, too" (379). In its worldly understanding and sense of justice, Sophia's summing-up recalls the French lieutenant's appraisal of Jim:

> There are evil moments in every life. A false suggestion enters one's brain, and then fear is born—fear of oneself, fear for oneself. Or else a false courage—who knows? Well, call it what you like; but tell me, how many of them would deliver themselves up deliberately to perdition (as he himself says in that book) rather than go on living, secretly debased in their own eyes? How many? . . . And please mark this—he was safe when he did it. It was just when he believed himself safe and more—infinitely more—when the possibility of being loved by that admirable girl first dawned upon him, that he discovered that his bitterest railings, the worst wickedness, the devil work of his hate and pride, could never cover up the ignominy of the existence before him. There's character in such a discovery. (379–80)

IV

SIGNIFICANT parallels between Razumov and the historical Prince Roman Sanguszko (1800–1881),[13] who is unchanged essentially in Conrad's story bearing his name written shortly after *Under Western Eyes*, suggest that the Polish prince served Conrad as a model of integrity for Razumov. This integrity, embracing Conrad's most esteemed qualities of character, subserves an ideal of patriotism. Personal ambition has no place. When Conrad's prince decides to enlist in the 1830 rebellion against the Russians, he tells his elderly confi-

dant, "There is no question here of leadership and glory. I mean to
go alone and to fight obscurely in the ranks" (43). Razumov's confession to his enemies resembles the prince's heroic bearing before the
Russian commission judging him for treason. As a former imperial
guardsman and late ordnance officer to the emperor, the prince,
who fought incognito until his identity was disclosed inadvertently
after capture, knew that he faced the death penalty. At the supreme
moment of his life, he rejects the proffered opportunity of safety.
He refuses to characterize his taking up arms as blind recklessness,
a sudden impulse arising from grief over his wife's death. He will
not repudiate his actions with a public lie, damn them as irresponsible, admit to an unfelt remorse. In silence, he writes to his judges,
"I joined the national uprising from conviction" (52). Conviction as
well as remorse determine Razumov's unmasking at Laspara's house,
affirming himself by ending a protective dissimulation. His confession embodies a reflective opposition to revolt, living proof of his
political ethos and stance of independence. It is worth noting that
the actual Prince Roman dissented strenuously from the 1863 uprising. Conrad became one of its tragic victims because of his father's
radical activities, which resulted in his arrest in 1861 and penal exile.
"Prince Roman, himself, after his experience in Siberia and in the
Caucasus, was simply appalled by the prospect of another Polish attempt against the Russian colossus and did not hesitate to throw the
prestige of his great name in the balance in order to stop the young
enthusiasts from joining the January Rising. In the beginning of 1863
Roman stayed in Cracow where he was one of the most outspoken
and determined foes of the Insurrection."[14] Conrad might have found
support for his own hatred of revolution in the example of this most
patriotic of Poles. Punishment for the prince is particularly cruel and
humiliating, as the czar intervenes personally in the sentencing, in
effect one of "deferred death." The prince is exiled to Siberia and
ordered to walk the enormous distance chained to common criminals. "Stone deaf, his health broken," he is permitted readmittance
to Poland after twenty-five years.[15] In severity of consequence for
confession, in disability, and in return to his homeland, Razumov's
fate is striking in its similarity. The substance of Prince Roman's remaining years is devoted to aiding his countrymen, always guided by
a "simple wisdom, a high sense of honour, and the most scrupulous

conception of private and public probity" (54). Though "crippled, ill, getting weaker every day," the deaf Razumov also serves his country as an honored voice, a man of earned integrity speaking with intellectual and moral authority, a metaphor, one suspects, for Conrad the writer.

CHAPTER SEVEN

Conclusion

I

THE PROBLEM of integrity is central to Conrad's moral preoccupations, affording coherence and focus to his delineation of character,
following a logical development as he matures in his art. Many of
the patterns, conflicts, and motifs intrinsic to this question are evident in "Heart of Darkness." However disguised or sublimated, individualism is the usual spur to action in Conrad's men. Africa lures
Marlow because of his need to fulfill a secret ideal self-conception,
that of an adventurer capable of responsible work in the midst of
adversity. The voyager Marlow manifests qualities typical of a Conradian protagonist: callowness, a romantic outlook, that is, a self-protective way of seeing tinged with vanity and idealism, and a lack of
moral discernment. Marlow's feeling of impostorship—an uncertain,
illusory sense of identity—adds urgency and complexity to the entire
problem of integrity. It may help account for a strain in Conrad of
intense striving for an elevated self-image which is simultaneously a
struggle against a sense of nonentity associated with mediocrity and
inaction. The treatment of the imposture motif suggests further that
identity can never be assured, that a sounder basis for authenticity
may lie in some version of selflessness, in a commitment to moral

truth and spiritual values rather than to the realm of action. The Buddha image of Marlow as voice that frames the narrative proper points in this direction.

Although Conrad honors community codes, he more forcibly resists the sovereignty of external ethical authority. The hero may transgress the law or civilized norms, but guilt is not acknowledged nor remorse felt, if at all, unless he understands his act to be self-destructive, which is to say that for Conrad conscience is the ultimate judge of one's conduct. Self judges self independently, and self accounts for punishment. One use of the double is to dramatize the process of moral and psychological self-recognition. Employment in a ruthlessly exploitative business sullies Marlow despite the apparent innocence of his intention in getting appointed. Complicity in the questionable, even while the protagonist maintains an unstained self-regard, is a tension that runs throughout Conrad's best art. Complicity gives the lie to the hero's sense of virtue, creates a reality which exerts pressure on his superiority and detachment.

The psychological climax of "Heart of Darkness" is Marlow's profound disillusionment, a collapse of values leading to disbelief, the extinction of self, and despair that hovers on the edge of suicide. In varying degrees of severity, duration, and seriousness of consequence, disillusionment strikes virtually every major Conradian figure. Disillusionment prepares one for knowledge, and how the character responds to the reality now exposed is crucial to the question of integrity. Marlow's renewal is bound up indissolubly with Kurtz. Remaining faithful to the dead man forces Marlow to dissociate himself morally from the company. The loyalty and debt one owes the doppelgänger stems basically from two sources: the other lives out one's worst possible fate, and he inspires one to grow into a higher self. Regeneration culminates in Marlow replacing Kurtz as a voice, in his transformation from seaman to storyteller. The integrity that Conrad is reaching for and whose outlines are adumbrated in "Heart of Darkness" is an independence that involves merging with and moral separation from the double and self-realization.

Conrad's conception of integrity emerges from the conflict between his belief in the self-affirming possibilities of action and his tragic vision. So withering is Conrad's skepticism and the tragic consciousness which is its outgrowth that even Conrad at times shies away from its implications. A pulling back is evident in the gallant lie Marlow tells the Intended and, complicated by Conrad's irony, in Marlow's overdrawn claims for the value of work. These questionable affirmations suggest that Conrad is unable as yet to surrender certain aspects of his romanticism: a need to retain a chivalrous attitude toward women, which serves a self-protective function, and a need to cling to definite moral statements, "ideals," which are undercut by his art. Nevertheless, "Heart of Darkness" advances enlargement of mind as a primary component of integrity. Egotistical action does not lead to the realization of identity but rather to its undermining, even to its loss. Integrity must have a moral dimension that subordinates and absorbs individualism. Consciousness by itself, inimical to action, is insufficient. "Heart of Darkness" is a relentless unmasking, a penetrating assault on values and ideas, including the very notion of "character," one's assumption of an independent personality. After this compelling deromanticization, what action is now possible, what kind of life follows? Given the seeming finality of this impasse, one problem Conrad faces is the formulation of a countervailing affirmation. In subsequent fiction this dilemma will become acute, particularly in the resolution of his protagonists' fates and in the endings of those works.

The deep pessimism that prevails in the novella is lightened in *Lord Jim*, so that the novel may be said to constitute a retreat from the tragic spirit of the Congo tale. Conrad's impulse is to spare Jim the disillusionment that Marlow suffered in the short story. Growth of mind would destroy Jim as a romantic character. Desperately maintaining his heroic self-image after the *Patna* safeguards him from despair, leaves Jim morally blind and vexed by conflict but keeps alive his fighting spirit. Fed by egotism and shame, Jim's flight from the Western community and from unnerving reminders is also a groping search for rehabilitation. In the Patusan section, Jim endeavors to win redemption through action even while Conrad recognizes its inadequacy and acknowledges the inevitable necessity for punishment. High accomplishments do not in themselves constitute the atonement and effective moral growth that resolve guilt.

Jim's misplaced allegiance to Brown in releasing him proceeds from crippling identification with the outcast and amounts to a repetition of his *Patna* irresponsibility. To preserve Jim as a romantic ideal, Conrad backs off from dramatizing his coming-to-knowledge be-

cause Conrad associates such a process with disintegration. That Jim
dies virtually untouched emotionally and physically suggests that
Conrad is keeping his hands off him, as it were. Although Jim seems
to triumph in his own eyes, a self-centeredness that must be weighed
against Jewel's abandonment and Brown's half-mad sense of victory
as he expires, the element of self-glorification in Jim's death, his defiance, and proud silence call attention to the moral limitations of
his self-chosen punishment/affirmation. Thus, the ambiguity and
criticism of this final act make Jim and his romantic claims problematic, an opening which leaves room for the future Nostromo.

Nostromo amplifies and extends the possibilities for attaining integrity. Disillusionment assails the novel's four leading male characters
as well as Emilia, and except for Decoud, betrayal and guilt figure
in the lives of the four other protagonists. The failures of Charles
Gould, Decoud, and Nostromo stem from egotism, romantic illusions, and insufficient faith. Integrity is realized partially in Emilia
and Monygham, which results largely from their selflessness, service,
and capacity to see the worst unflinchingly. The hope of efficiency,
advanced but mocked by the reality in "Heart of Darkness," is brought
to fulfillment by Charles and the silver mine. However, victory is
seriously flawed, for it promotes a new injustice and instability. Even
if imbued with patriotic feeling and heroic imagination, work cannot
support a transcendent creed because it is based on materialism.
Inevitably, the mine comes to possess the mine owner. By his failure,
Gould helps prepare for the integrity Conrad reaches in *Under Western Eyes*, rooted as it is in a selfless patriotism divorced from mater-
ialistic activity.

Emilia is Conrad's finest portrait of a woman, and while he avoids
the condescension and overprotectiveness of sentimentality, he tends
to idealize her, giving her an aura of nobility which prevents her
from becoming a completely living woman. Within traditional fem-
inine boundaries of self-sacrifice, devotion to husband, and communal engagement, she bears the fullest burden of suffering. She
sees tragic reality as does Monygham, but she retains her humanity
and does not insist on truth at the expense of compassion. However,
no independence and affirmation is within her reach because she is
a loyal wife bound to honor her national prestige, because foreign
birth and European sensibility separate her from the true spirit of
the country, and because she has no far-reaching political vision. In

just these areas where Emilia is blocked, Natalie of *Under Western Eyes* has the possibilities that enable her to realize a higher integrity as a woman.

Decoud and Monygham play out two versions of Conrad's extreme skepticism. The life of the dilettante and sophisticate in Paris has spoiled Decoud with a luxury of idle freedom. Though Antonia helps draw him back to his homeland and into its struggles, Decoud never loses this soft spot, which proves his undoing. Formidable as it is, Decoud's skeptical intelligence is not an outgrowth of personal travail, and so it costs him nothing. A disparity exists between his penetrating mind and a tenderness of heart. Unsentimental but callow, he is ignorant of his absolute dependence on society, unaware of the fragility of individuality. He has neither firmness of character nor faith to resist the corrosive pressure of skepticism in isolation. Love for Antonia and patriotism prove to be illusions generated by egotism and not sustaining beliefs. Neither can inspire a life-saving impulse to counteract the desolation and terror that crush him on the Great Isabel. With Decoud, Conrad forces to a logical conclusion the deadly opposition between consciousness and egotism.

In Monygham, Conrad traces the prolonged effects of disillusionment and remorse. After imprisonment, betrayal under torture, and years of self-imposed exile in the wilds, Monygham is damaged emotionally, stripped of egotism, and left with a skepticism that has calcified into misanthropy. While his inner toughness saves him where Decoud snaps and Nostromo sinks into corruption, his sources of feeling have been impaired. Remorse is especially ravaging in Conrad, and Monygham endures its full brunt with no hope of release. Only he condemns himself for his past deed. If not for Emilia, he would remain trapped in self-laceration and despair, wasting himself in poverty. Monygham and Emilia prefigure Razumov and Natalie in that an admirable and lovely woman, who inspires an idealized love, induces the embittered hero to courageous action that leads to self-transcendence. However, one aspect of Monygham's limitation is his strain of self-abasement and fanaticism, evident in his worship of Mrs. Gould and in his enmity toward Nostromo. Cut loose from society, the doctor speaks with a trenchant independence of mind. Though Monygham's intelligence is an instrument of truth, it is a nihilistic force, the principle of ruthless exposure. Monygham can penetrate appearance with a chilling incisiveness, but he can envision nothing better, can neither inspire, enrich, nor console. While Conrad grants him personal redemption, the recovery of self-respect, no larger affirmation can come from him. Monygham's disengagement is born of the tragic resignation that carries great authority for Conrad, profoundly different from Decoud's aloofness or Razumov's complacent retirement. However, resignation in Conrad coexists with a tension to find affirming action which does not falsify tragic knowledge or rely on egotistical claims, a tension that is resolved dramatically only in *Under Western Eyes*.

Nostromo is Conrad's fullest elaboration of the romantic ideal, the man bound utterly to an heroic self-conception. The adolescent glory for which Jim yearned reaches a finished stage in the Italian's extraordinary conceit. Remarkable for his abilities and his exploits, Nostromo is all vanity, so that his allegiance has no moral underpinnings. By portraying his helpless, shabby debasement, Conrad advances beyond Jim, who elected death when his world crumbled in Patusan. Importantly, Nostromo's decline sets in before he seizes the treasure. Isolation, the sense of failure, awakened thought, and deprivation of an admiring public so shake him that his very personality slips away. Although not a principal offense in Conrad's moral hierarchy, Nostromo's theft is intentional, clandestine, and unambiguous. The nature of the crime makes guilt conscious and redemption impossible. Conrad's reluctance to kill his Capataz is apparent in the perfunctoriness of his suffering, the inept and melodramatic manner of death. Nostromo's love complications and punishment comprise the novel's worst writing, suggesting Conrad's difficulty in relinquishing romantic claims. Nostromo is incapable of moral growth, confirming that romanticism and integrity are irreconcilable. However, Conrad must still exert unsparing critical pressure on his romantic figure of action, a problem mastered in the treatment of Haldin. At the same time, the resourceful, enterprising male lives on in Leggatt, a Nostromo deromanticized.

II

AS ROMANTIC complement to *Under Western Eyes*, "The Secret Sharer" provides a vital openness, possibility, and affirmation that allow Conrad to deal directly with a work that carries the full burden of tragedy.

Rare in Conrad's best art, the optimistic note on which the maritime piece ends is that of youth moving ahead confidently; in the conclusion to the Russian novel, which Conrad resumed after he finished "The Secret Sharer," Razumov is barred from the future and action. The novice shipmaster inhabits a Conradian universe familiar in its harshness and pessimism, but while dark elements press in, they never quite overwhelm the promise that Conrad fights for and wins. Several factors account for the assurance Conrad can share qualifiedly with his sanguine commander. Trust between the doubles is upheld and proves mutually life-giving. Identification with their professional roles serves to contain, if not eliminate, self-aggrandizing tendencies, and neither officer is restless for glory, adventure, or heroism. Equally important, consciousness is beyond them. The storyteller's simplicity and immediate concerns rule out reflection, so that what is fearful and disturbing in his narrative never penetrates to the level of thoughtful articulation. An absence of doubt makes possible and keeps intact his surge of good feeling after the Koh-ring maneuver, a necessary trial. While his hopeful assessment of Leggatt's prospects is overstated, it does have a firm basis, though for considerations outside his grasp. Thus, the story preserves and advances those values of leadership that make for successful action.

Deftly and with cause, Conrad shields Leggatt from remorse. The circumstances and nature of the crime make self-censure improbable, nor is the first mate given to inwardness, deliberation, or self-mistrust. Moreover, Leggatt's violent aggression is allied inextricably with his initiative and valor. The story's tragic brunt descends on Archbold. Even before Leggatt's engagement, the old skipper had abdicated authority, and during the gale he loses heart and retreats from responsibility. Judged by internal standards, the conscience-stricken Archbold is damned. By afflicting the *Sephora*'s captain with guilt feelings and by using doubles to resolve the theme of redemption, Conrad establishes the conditions whereby the narrator can earn a limited integrity. Leggatt's freedom is sufficiently hard to be considered simultaneously as punishment. Conrad's working out of guilt demands also redemption, duplicating the conditions of the transgressive deed where now the offender behaves with courage and responsibility. Succeeding in his emergency by luck and disciplined response where Leggatt had failed, the newcomer proves himself worthy and symbolically redeems his lapsed double. Achieving captaincy also confirms the spiritual "legacy" of the chief mate. Sympathetically, Leggatt has bequeathed to his untried brother officer and unfallen self the inspiration and example necessary to realize his vocation. The initiate becomes the wished-for ideal by merging with and transcending morally the experienced model.

Having won an integrity of action in "The Secret Sharer," Conrad is able to give *Under Western Eyes* its necessary tragic dimensions. The novel treats in definitive terms betrayal and guilt. Tantamount to murder, Razumov's infidelity to Haldin is the only time Conrad dramatizes explicitly the intentional betrayal of the double in his open appeal for trust. No mitigating circumstances obtain because the treachery is calculated. The wrongness of the act resides in its cowardice, in its desecration of the spirit of patriotism, and in its self-destructiveness, for in crushing a perceived antagonist, Razumov strikes against his unawakened humanity. Haldin's fate conforms to Conrad's most uncompromising pattern of disillusionment, remorse, and self-sought punishment. Compelled to grasp that his visit is a monstrous violation, the now guilt-ridden revolutionary eschews flight and exposes himself knowingly to certain capture. Conrad grants Haldin, an embodiment of personal political hatreds, consciousness and dignity as he meets his end, for the condemned man refuses to incriminate Razumov in retaliation.

The theme of imposture receives its most subtle and comprehensive development. In Conrad's Russia, the supremacy of politics dooms romantic action. Identity rests on political conscience that must be professed, a burden from which Razumov shrinks. Unwittingly, Razumov acquires an undeserved reputation for trustworthiness and profundity, and Haldin's further glamorization of this image leads the terrorist to choose him as confidant and agent of escape. By going first to Ziemianitch and then to the authorities, Razumov compromises his independence. Prince K—and Mikulin use him as Razumov's need for sympathy becomes a means of inducing him to collaborate in his own seduction. Consequently, he falls into a corrupt existence, submitting to the imposed fictitious identities of revolutionary hero and state supporter/police agent.

Haldin's posthumous influence on Razumov is to infiltrate his psyche, to shape his character and fate. Circumstance dictates that

Razumov allow himself to become Haldin's appendage, compatriot, and finally, replacement. But because Razumov is the weaker spiritually, he loses himself increasingly in Haldin's identity. Impersonation suffocates him in a horrible falseness. Contamination, inescapable self-loathing, and debasement of soul war against his lust for vengeance, the evil design of which is to possess Natalie. But Razumov is touched by the Haldin family and by Victor's spirit working through them. Haldin has been canonized as patriot and martyr, so that his own rage against Victor cannot be revenged. Razumov grasps that surrending the assassin was self-destructive in that he has robbed himself of a life of his own. Not betraying again by confessing to Natalie symbolically undoes the original perfidy. Confession to the radicals is essential to assuage guilt, profess autonomy, and accept punishment. Victor's legacy has been to elevate Razumov's soul through suffering, to inspire him to discover and embrace conscience. Purged of egotism, Razumov merges with Haldin by coming to serve the spirit of patriotism, yet separates from the extremist by being transformed into an honored, independent, tragic voice. Razumov's doomed heroism means repudiation of the world, yet this tragic stature encompasses an affirmation not possible for any other major Conradian figure. Returned to his homeland, a crippled Razumov speaks to and for his countrymen, a metaphoric ideal for the author as patriotic voice. Conrad's art can reach no higher conception of integrity.

A Note on *Victory*: Disbelief and Depletion

WITH *Under Western Eyes* Conrad achieved a resolution of major proportions whose consequences for his art were extreme. With the
qualified exception of "The Shadow Line," a conservative and diluted reworking of material in "The Secret Sharer," Conrad's fiction
after *Under Western Eyes* is decidedly inferior. What Heyst says of himself to Lena, "No force or conviction," can be said equally for *Victory*.
The book lacks power. Heyst is the expression of Conrad's exhaustion of belief in self-authenticating action. Might not one see in Heyst's
powerlessness the logical extension of Razumov's doomed heroism?
Depleted individualism takes the form of "gentlemanliness" in Heyst,
humane impulse attenuated by an excessive delicacy of sensibility.
Heyst's insubstantiality feeds his mistrust of life and accounts largely
for his passive renunciation. In varying degrees Conrad's chief male
characters often demonstrate passivity, detachment, and skepticism,
but simultaneously they have a vitality that presupposes an inner
connection to the world. Specifically, Heyst's precursors Decoud,
Monygham, and Razumov do act despite resistance and act effectively for a time. But Heyst's difference from these men is more than
one of degree. Although this Swedish exile comes closest in Conrad
to a recluse, the trouble is, remarks Davidson, Heyst is not a hermit
by temperament. An innate decency prompts intervention, yet while

Heyst can rescue others, he obviously cannot defend himself. However, it is not decency but passion and conviction that move Conrad's heroes to significant action. When love is involved, it is more chaste or unfulfilled than sexual, and it is never love alone that forces engagement. The Swede, however, is without passionate conviction, and he lacks a vital core of being that would make of his love a self-transcending emotion.

Heyst enters the novel with a fundamental and fatal defect, a deficiency of spirit which renders him as incapable of corruption as of moral growth. Whatever explains this impairment (the influence of a misanthropic philosopher father is stressed), it admits of no remedy upon which Conrad can call. Dramatic conflict cannot develop, for it is soon evident that nothing will bring Heyst alive. Want of self-pride, ambition, and faith make him a defeated man to begin with. Despite robustness and a knightlike appearance ("in the fulness of his physical development, of a broad, martial presence, with his bald head and long moustaches, he resembled the portraits of Charles XII, of adventurous memory"), "there was no reason to think that Heyst was in any way a fighting man" (9). Primarily because he is without fighting spirit, Heyst's chivalry is of no account, is in fact a liability. Although Conrad does not locate Heyst as a product of modern forces, he is recognizable as a modern type of antihero: passive, marked by disbelief, alienation, and a sense of helplessness before the world, as well as weakened by a diminished emotional capacity. Heyst's plan to pass unscathed through life never has sufficient justification. Inherited from his father, his disenchantment is not earned independently through painful experience, so that his outlook lacks conviction and depth. Not only is his compassion at odds with his aloofness, but his nature is too fragile to support the skeptical attitude he posits. A man who holds that the world is a bad dog that will bite given the chance caves in rather quickly when that reality breaks through in the form of Schomberg's calumny. Heyst's "soft" social sense reveals itself in this hypersensitive regard for reputation, in his exorbitant need for a scrupulous self-image. One reason he advances for not defending himself against the invaders is the villainy outsiders will read into his conduct, which is to carry Prufrock's self-deprecatory lament, "Do I dare to eat a peach?" to a suicidal extreme. Though the baron is not a coward, his innocence, ineptitude, and meekness are appalling. Contact is equated with contamination, and even with Lena, Heyst's overconcern with purity, his fastidiousness, shows itself in a reluctance to touch and be touched.

Admittedly, it is difficult to write an absorbing work of some length about a passive figure, but Heyst is weakly rendered in a weak novel. Episodes designed to suggest his impoverishment are insubstantial in themselves. For example, in "Heart of Darkness" and *Nostromo*, respectively, Conrad is masterful in evoking penetration into a jungle interior and in treating a mining venture meant to carry progress into a dormant area. Conrad resurrects this material briefly in *Victory* as if to confirm that the great experiences which had dominated his earlier heroes can have no appreciable impact on Heyst, but this novelistic terrain now seems dead to Conrad also. Restless wandering takes Heyst to the cannibal-inhabited regions of New Guinea, where, we are to believe, he had encountered "the most exciting of his earlier futile adventures" (82). For a man who claims to have been immersed in hardship and peril, Heyst is disappointingly inarticulate to Lena:

> My dear girl, you don't know the sort of life I have been leading in unexplored countries, in the wilds; it's difficult to give you an idea. There are men who haven't been in such tight places as I have found myself in who have had to—to shed blood, as the saying is. Even the wilds hold prizes which tempt some people; but I had no schemes, no plans—and not even great firmness of mind to make me unduly obstinate. I was simply moving on, while the others, perhaps, were going somewhere. An indifference as to roads and purposes makes one meeker, as it were. (211–12)

That he was unaffected in any way is simply not credible, and aimlessness will hardly do as explanation. Returning to civilization after a long absence, a portfolio of sketches underarm implying a cultured detachment, Heyst remarks only that he had had "an amusing time." Evidently, Conrad wants to indicate an impaired capacity to engage and respond to challenge, but Heyst seems to have experienced hardly at all. It is not merely as if he had not gone to New Guinea, but imaginatively Conrad has not sent him. "Realistically" and psychologically, New Guinea is miles apart from Samburan, but in *Victory* they seem of a piece. Heyst's timidity may be reflected in the gentleness of his island, but Conrad's unimpressive evocation of landscape betrays diminished powers. Character, environment, conflict, irony, and intellectual content have been domesticated.

In every way the Tropical Belt Coal Company is a pale glimmer of the San Tomé Mine, a rich artistic vein played out. In his impractical business sense and want of staying power, the Swede resembles Gould's hapless father. With the project's collapse, Heyst's divorce from hard facts is not so much occasioned by dashed prospects or financial loss as it is meant to show bankruptcy of vision. The "great stride forward" that inspired his short outburst of industry is a feeble echo of Gould's expansive and stirring hopes. The power of silver that pervades *Nostromo* shrivels to a foolhardy scheme of tropical coal, a soon insolvent operation, a man whose initiative runs out at the first setback, a trio of incompetent desperadoes chasing a rumor of treasure.

Despite the large position love assumes in the novel, Conrad has no belief in the possibilities of mature heterosexual love to affirm selfhood. Whereas a preposterous magnanimity and sexual repression combine to emasculate Anthony of *Chance*, physical intimacy does nothing to awaken self-pride in the Swede. Pathetically, nothing can be done with Heyst, a truth implicit in his last words: "Ah, Davidson, woe to the man whose heart has not learned while young to hope, to love—and to put its trust in life" (410). With its suggestion of self-pity and helplessness, this simple, pious, and sentimental message carries no authority. *Victory* only half-heartedly addresses the problem of how this trust is to be acquired. It is true that the book urges activity, self-assertion, and love, but this appeal is realized superficially and never rises above the conventional. The tragedy of Conrad's universe, where the struggle for affirmation was enacted in the most extreme terms, has been reduced to melodrama. The tragic sense that concludes *Lord Jim* and most impressively *Under Western Eyes* is entirely absent here. Davidson's "Nothing," which closes the tale, rather than sounding a tragic note, is a lame reminder of Heyst's emptiness and intimates that the victory in the novel is Conrad's disbelief.

Notes

1. Introduction

1. See, for example, Morton Dauwen Zabel, "Conrad," in his *Craft and Character in Modern Fiction* (New York: Viking, 1957), pp. 147–227; includes revised version of his "Joseph Conrad: Chance and Recognition," *Sewanee Review* 53 (Winter 1945): 1–22; John Palmer, *Joseph Conrad's Fiction* (Ithaca, N.Y.: Cornell University Press, 1968).

2. Edward Garnett, ed., *Letters from Joseph Conrad 1895–1924* (1928; rpt. Indianapolis: Bobbs-Merrill Charter Books, 1962), p. 8.

3. Conrad to Poradowski, Friday, [20 July? 1894], Frederick R. Karl and Lawrence Davis, eds., *The Collected Letters of Joseph Conrad, vol. I, 1861–1897* (Cambridge: Cambridge University Press, 1983), pp. 162–63.

4. Albert J. Guerard, *Conrad the Novelist* (Cambridge, Mass.: Harvard University Press, 1958), pp. 1–59.

5. Irving Howe, "Introduction: The Idea of the Modern," in *The Idea of the Modern in Literature and the Arts*, ed. Irving Howe (New York: Horizon Press, 1967), pp. 11–40.

6. Howe, "Idea of the Modern," p. 39. In addition to the acceptance as fact, as given, of a godless universe (whose consequences are extreme), these qualities, among others, Howe identifies as comprising the modernist spirit in literature: an uncompromising complexity, a devotion to the problematic, a persistent, unrelieved questioning and stripping down, particularly of established values and norms, technical innovation and experimentation, an intensification of the values of self, a preoccupation with psychic inwardness, an extreme subjectivity of outlook, an insistence on sincerity and authentic response, and a heightened emphasis on making visible the writer's reality. Among important modernist writers, modernist in various degrees, Howe includes Conrad, Mann, Kafka, Proust, Gide, Malraux, Lawrence, Brecht, Yeats, Eliot, Joyce, and Beckett.

The major moral critics of Conrad who, by assumption or implication, whether deliberately or tacitly, treat him in large measure as modernist are: David Daiches, *The Novel and the Modern World* (1939; rev. ed. Chicago: University of Chicago Press, 1965); Morton Dauwen Zabel, "Conrad," in his *Craft and Character* and his Introduction to *The Portable Conrad*, ed. Zabel (New York: Viking, 1947), pp. 1–47; Irving Howe, *Politics and the Novel* (New York: Horizon Press and Meridian Books, 1957); Albert J. Guerard, *Conrad the Novelist* (Cambridge, Mass.: Harvard University Press, 1958); J. Hillis Miller, *Poets of Reality* (1965; rpt. New York: Atheneum, 1969), pp. 13–67; and Lionel Trilling, *Sincerity and Authenticity* (Cambridge, Mass.: Harvard University Press, 1971). Although Trilling discusses Conrad briefly, his book is relevant because it traces the concept of selfhood historically, with special emphasis on its nature and possibilities in the modern world.

A recent moral critic who treats Conrad as a modernist is Suresh Raval, *The Art of Failure: Conrad's Fiction* (Boston: Allen and Unwin, 1986). His study emphasizes the interplay between private ideals and a particular community, the impact of political and socioeconomic forces on character, the difficulties in establishing the authority of Conrad's narrators, and problems of truth and understanding involving language. But even where Raval sees despair "as the inalienable element within understanding" in Conrad (17) and considers him a tragic writer, his exposition of Conrad's values and art is not carried far enough. Raval tends not to favor character analysis, and he avoids linking Conrad's life and fiction, two areas that can help reveal a work's depth and range and its place in Conrad's career.

7. This orientation is found in F. R. Leavis, *The Great Tradition* (1948; rpt. Garden City, N.Y.: Doubleday Anchor, 1954). Other important critics include Ian Watt, "Joseph Conrad: Alienation and Commitment," in *The English Mind: Studies in the English Moralists Presented to Basil Wiley*, ed. Hugh Sykes Davies and George Watson (Cambridge: Cambridge University Press, 1964), pp. 257–78; Avrom Fleishman, *Conrad's Politics: Community and Anarchy in the Fiction of Joseph Conrad* (Baltimore: The John Hopkins University Press, 1967); David Thorburn, *Conrad's Romanticism* (New Haven: Yale University Press, 1974), and among the archetypal critics who examine moral patterns I include as representative Claire Rosenfield, *Paradise of Snakes: An Archetypal Analysis of Conrad's Political Novels* (Chicago: University of Chicago Press, 1967).

Daniel Schwarz, a recent critic in this conservative mold, takes a humanistic approach, which gives less credence to Conrad's pessimism and nihilism: *Conrad: "Almayer's Folly" to "Under Western Eyes"* (Ithaca, N.Y.: Cornell University Press, 1980). Aside from the familiar Conradian ideals of fidelity, courage, solidarity, and work, Schwarz stresses as a major theme in Conrad the importance of restoring personal and family ties. And in the later work, according to Schwarz, Conrad emphasized private virtues, such as "consideration for others, tact, sensitivity, flexibility, and tenderness" (xvii). But Schwarz's efforts to elevate Conrad's humanism has its costs. He takes insufficient account of Conrad's skepticism, of the elements of opposition within individual texts, so that the affirmations he claims for Conrad are established too easily. See also Schwarz, *Conrad: The Later Fiction* (London: Macmillan, 1982).

8. Zdzislaw Najder, *Joseph Conrad: A Chronicle* (New Brunswick, N.J.: Rutgers University Press, 1983), p. 222. See also Zdzislaw Najder, *Conrad Under Familial Eyes*, trans. Halina Carroll-Najder (Cambridge: Cambridge University Press, 1984) and Zdzislaw Najder, *Conrad's Polish Background: Letters to and from Polish Friends.* (London: Oxford University Press, 1964).

9. Najder, *A Chronicle*, p. 221.

10. In his essay "Books," Conrad denies the charge of nihilism often levelled against him. Despite its elegant formality, these words do not misrepresent Conrad's own fiction: "It must not be supposed that I claim for the artist in fiction the freedom of moral Nihilism. I would require from him many acts of faith of which the first would be the cherishing of an undying hope. . . . To be hopeful in an artistic sense it is not necessary to think that the world is good. It is enough to believe that there is no impossibility of its being made so" (*Notes on Life and Letters* [London: J. M. Dent, 1949], pp. 8–9).

11. Frederic Jameson's Marxist literary analysis minimizes ethical criticism, which he views as an allegorical rewriting of a given text according to a master code which "projects as permanent features of human 'experience,' thus as a kind of 'wisdom' about personal life and interpersonal relations, what are in reality the historical and institutional specifics of a determinate type of group solidarity or cohesion" (*The Political Unconsciousness* [Ithaca, N.Y.: Cornell University Press, 1981], p. 59). Given his ideological presuppositions and aims, Jameson's Marxist reading of Conrad, primarily *Nostromo*, is not finely attuned to esthetic questions or to the psychological and moral subtleties raised by Conrad's characters, areas of particular concern to me.

12. Focusing on forms of repetition that he sees as integral to *Lord Jim*'s self-interpretive process, J. Hillis Miller's deconstructionist reading of the novel finds ambiguity, indeterminacy, and equivocalness of meaning to pervade and dominate the work (*Fiction and Repetition: Seven English Novels* [Cambridge: Harvard University Press, 1982], pp. 22–41). However, where Miller cancels the author and excludes comparisons with other Conradian works, I do not. One reason for the novel's ambiguity, I propose, has to do with Conrad's complicated attitude toward Jim. Here, ambiguity functions as a distancing principle and as a protective device. Conrad wants to keep a heroic dimension to Jim even as punishment must be inevitable and final. By sparing Jim the full rigor of his skepticism, which would bring consciousness and remorse to a character unable to endure their effects, Conrad preserves romantic possibilities for himself. Additionally, by comparing *Lord Jim* with *Under Western Eyes*, I argue that the absence of ambiguity in the later novel is indicative of Conrad's artistic maturation. It clarifies in what ways Jim fails to gain the moral stature Razumov earns.

Another deconstructionist critic, Perry Meisel, argues that "Heart of Darkness" is not a psychological text but one which "interrogates the epistemological status of the language in which it inheres," which severs the actual links between the literary text and the conditions of the real world: "Decentering *Heart of Darkness*," *Modern Language Studies* 8, no. 3 (1978): 20–28. With the "shift or recession of centers that makes up the drama of Marlow's search" (23), Meisel suggests "that the horror that assails Marlow has to do with the impossibility of disclosing a central core, an essence, even a ground to what Kurtz has done and what he is" (25). However, from my perspective the more important focus is Marlow and what Kurtz signifies for him. Marlow's identification with his double means that Kurtz's blankness, his emptiness at the core, is also Marlow's interior vacancy, an absence of a secure identity. This recognition of his own horror within leads to a dissolution of self. Identity is an illusion, a social construct, capable of being lost under extremity. But the tale does not stop here with a center of meaninglessness; it adumbrates Marlow's process of self-renewal. He undergoes a transformation from seaman to storyteller, reflecting Conrad's own assumption of a new self from mariner to serious novelist.

13. The most persuasive analysis of this aspect of Conrad's career is Thomas Moser, *Joseph Conrad: Achievement and Decline* (Cambridge: Harvard University Press, 1957).

Moser demonstrates Conrad's change of attitude and approach after *Under Western Eyes*, the emergence of a sentimental ethic, giving as partial answers for this shift a quest for popularity, a need to change from moral themes, and a desire to write of love, most notably in *Chance*.

2. "Heart of Darkness": Loss of Self

1. Many critics have noted that Marguerite Poradowski, wife of Conrad's distant relative Aleksander Poradowski, helped Conrad secure a position with the Société Anonyme Belge pour le Commerce du Haut-Congo, e.g., Zdzislaw Najder, *Joseph Conrad: A Chronicle* (New Brunswick, N.J.: Rutgers University Press, 1983), p. 118ff., Frederick R. Karl, *Joseph Conrad: The Three Lives* (New York: Farrar, Straus and Giroux, 1979), p. 276ff.

2. "Heart of Darkness" in *Youth: A Narrative and Two Other Stories*, p. 59. All references to Conrad's works are to the Collected Edition (London: J. M. Dent, 1946–55), unless otherwise specified.

3. Conrad's "Congo Diary" consists of two notebooks written in pencil. The second and longer book contains only technical notes on navigation. Eloise Knapp Hay thinks that the fictional Towser book was suggested by Alfred Henry Alston's manual of seamanship, one of Conrad's favorite books which he kept from his own training days (*The Political Novels of Joseph Conrad* [Chicago: University of Chicago Press, 1963], p. 144n). However, that Conrad compiled navigational data while in the Congo suggests a frame of mind similar to Marlow's. This episode in the story, then, seems to be another example of Conrad's self-irony. Witness Marlow's comment: "Fancy a man lugging with him a book of that description into this nowhere and studying it—and making notes—in cipher at that!"

4. *The Mirror of the Sea and A Personal Record*, p. xvii.

5. Preface to *A Personal Record*, p. xviii.

6. Albert J. Guerard, *Conrad the Novelist* (Cambridge: Harvard University Press, 1958), p. 47.

7. R. D. Laing, *The Divided Self* (Baltimore: Penguin Books, 1965), p. 39ff.

8. In "Geography and Some Explorers" Conrad eulogizes the spirit of exploration and adventure, a spirit he associates with Mungo Park, Bruce, and Livingstone, and with which he identified from boyhood. By 1890, however, the heroic ideal had been debased by the greed and commercialism of those who came after the early African explorers. Conrad recalls his sense of disillusion and futility when he reached the Upper Congo:

> I said to myself with awe, 'This is the very spot of my boyhood boast.'
> A great melancholy descended on me. Yes, this was the very spot. But there was no shadowy friend to stand by my side in the night of enormous wilderness, no great haunting memory, but only the unholy recollection of a prosaic newspaper 'stunt' and the distasteful knowledge of the vilest scramble for loot that ever disfigured the history of human conscience and geographical exploration. What an end to the idealised realities of a boy's daydreams! I wondered what I was doing there, for indeed it was only an unforeseen episode, hard to believe in now, in my seaman's life. Still, the fact remains that I have smoked a pipe of peace at midnight in the very heart of the African continent, and felt very lonely there. (*Last Essays*, p. 25)

In "Travel" Conrad alludes to the passing of an heroic era, and he holds up for admiration those qualities exemplified by the early explorers and affirmed in his fiction.

The world of explorers and discoverers, the heroes of my boyhood, has vanished almost to nothing in the nineteenth century. . . . but no passage of years can dim my admiration for their selfless spirit and manly faithfulness to their task pursued in solitude or with a few devoted henchmen, persevered in through numberless days with death only a pace behind, but with a calm mind and a steady heart. (*Last Essays,* p. 126)

9. Because of the Russian occupation of Poland, Conrad was a Russian citizen until the Russian Ministry of Home Affairs released him from the status of Russian subject on March 31, 1889. Over three months later the official announcement was published in *Senatskye Vyedomsti* of St. Petersburg. Najder, *A Chronicle,* p. 112; Jocelyn Baines, *Joseph Conrad: A Critical Biography* (New York: McGraw-Hill, 1960), p. 101. Conrad became a naturalized British subject in 1886. See also Karl, *The Three Lives,* p. 274.

3. *Lord Jim*: Romantic Retreat

1. *Lord Jim,* p. 98.

2. Albert J. Guerard, *Conrad the Novelist* (Cambridge, Mass.: Harvard University Press, 1958), p. 147.

3. Morton Dauwen Zabel, Introduction, *Lord Jim* (Cambridge, Mass.: Riverside Press, 1958), p. xxii.

4. The creative periods of both works interpenetrate and overlap. Amidst other projects, Conrad started "Heart of Darkness" in mid-December of 1898 (apparently he had put aside work on *Lord Jim*) and finished it in about a month. Zdzislaw Najder, *Joseph Conrad: A Chronicle* (New Brunwick, N.J.: Rutgers University Press, 1983), pp. 249–50; Frederick R. Karl, *Joseph Conrad: The Three Lives* (New York: Farrar, Straus and Giroux, 1979), p. 439ff.). *Lord Jim* had begun to take shape as a short story in the spring of 1898 and was completed in July 1900 (Najder, *A Chronicle,* p. 265; Karl, *The Three Lives,* p. 502). Conrad seems to have had an imaginative necessity to "balance" dual and conflicting strains in his artistic temperament in separate major works. My chapter on "The Secret Sharer" discusses a more complicated expression of this pattern, where I argue that the maritime tale serves as a "romantic" complement to the "tragic" *Under Western Eyes.*

5. Dorothy Van Ghent, "On *Lord Jim*," in her *The English Novel: Form and Function* (1953; rpt. New York: Torchbooks–Harper & Row, 1961), p. 239.

6. In the case of the *Jeddha* upon which Conrad based his *Patna* episode, only Captain Joseph Lucas Clark was punished officially with a three-year certificate suspension, a penalty widely regarded to be lenient. For a thorough factual account, see Norman Sherry, *Conrad's Eastern World* (Cambridge: Cambridge University Press, 1966).

7. A recurring test of character in Conrad is one's capacity to resist the terrors of imagination, a vision of oneself suffering the fate one fears most, associated invariably with failure, desolation, exile, poverty, and futurelessness. This image can cause paralysis, panic that leads to cowardice, the haunting fear that corrodes one's vital confidence, or suicide. For example, Brierly finds the idea of his own failure intolerable; Nostromo cannot bear loss of reputation and a life of poverty; Decoud's resistance collapses on the Great Isabel when he senses his utter insignificance apart from society; the captain in "The Secret Sharer" glimpses a fearful image of himself wandering hatless under the pitiless sun of Koh-ring; and Razumov is demoralized at the prospect of a grubby future as a bureaucratic drudge in the Russian outskirts.

8. Gordon Allport, *Becoming* (New Haven: Yale University Press, 1955), p. 73.

9. Van Ghent, p. 237.

10. The restraint and undemonstrativeness of Conrad's mature men of courage was

much admired by Hemingway, many of whose own characters embody just such an attitude.

11. Guerard observes that "Conrad was unable to dramatize a projection of his artistic-intellectual self (as opposed to the adventurous-seaman self)" (p. 93).

12. Jocelyn Baines, *Joseph Conrad: A Critical Biography* (New York: McGraw-Hill, 1960), p. 250. Ian Watt also takes this view. See his *Conrad in the Nineteenth Century* (Berkeley: University of California Press, 1979), pp. 341–44, 353–54.

13. Gustav Morf, *The Polish Heritage of Joseph Conrad* (1930; rpt. New York: Haskell House, 1965), p. 158.

14. Van Ghent, p. 235.

15. Morf also reads Jim's comment on Brown as applying equally to himself (p. 158).

16. Guerard, *Conrad the Novelist*, p. 153.

17. A craven expression of Brown's passionate hatred of Jim is evident in Schomberg's malice toward the white-clad Heyst, whose air of aristocratic superiority and whose disinclination to patronize his hotel inflame the German to animosity.

18. Van Ghent, p. 235.

19. Guerard, *Conrad the Novelist*, p. 144. This reading of ambiguity in Jim's death is but one of many critical responses to its meaning. Karl dismisses Jim as a compulsive neurotic, removes him from the realm of the tragic, and prefers to consider him as the modern outsider. "Jim in his semi-articulate and stumbling way, in his sense of almost complete failure, in his inability to act powerfully and wisely, is a compelling guide to the modern temper; and his frustrated quest for personal salvation in an indifferent or hostile world is Conrad's distressing prophecy for the twentieth century" (*A Reader's Guide to Joseph Conrad*, rev. ed. [New York: Farrar, Straus and Giroux, 1969], p. 131). Baines holds that Jim's death constitutes a victory, for thereby he atones for the guilt attached to his *Patna* desertion. "An act of cowardice had to be expiated with the supreme act of courage, the deliberate going to meet certain death" (p. 252). For Tony Tanner, Jim's romantic idealism, evident in his death, makes him fallible and blameworthy, for it renders him incapable of pragmatic action in a crisis. Failure to deal effectively with Brown and submitting to Doramin's revenge instead of fighting reveal the passivity that is romanticism's fatal weakness. Man must learn to live in the world with all its baseness, "seeking only such honor as is consistent with an unremitting efficiency" (*Conrad: "Lord Jim"* [Woodbury, N.Y.: Barron's Educational Series, 1963], p. 56). Van Ghent sees Jim falling short of the classical tragic hero, doubting whether his ordeal of exile, guilt, and final loss has given him the knowledge, "and with the knowledge the nobility, which is the mysterious and sublime gift of suffering" (p. 231). In contrast, Watt argues that despite Jim's failure in self-knowledge, he does attain some of the moral grandeur of the tragic hero in confronting his destiny. Jim is faithful to the ideal of personal conduct found in medieval romance and dies for his honor. Conceding a certain boyishness in Jim's conception of chivalry, Watt does not see this immaturity as particularly damaging to Jim's final stature. Conrad "would have regarded a degree of intellectual callowness as a price well worth paying in exchange for fixed principles of honour" (p. 354). Watt elevates knightly honor over moral consciousness and considers Jim's death ennobling. Not only is Jim honorable in releasing Brown but his acceptance of death demonstrates courage, affirms friendship (with Dain), and expresses a keeping faith (with Stein), all values of the chivalric code. (See Watt, *Conrad in the Nineteenth Century*, pp. 338–56.)

20. In "The Secret Sharer" Leggatt, whose loss of control during a crisis causes him to kill a mutinous seaman, is initially described when swimming near the captain's

ship as a "headless corpse," and the story makes extensive symbolic use of a floppy hat.

21. "At present he was answering questions that did not matter though they had a purpose, but he doubted whether he would ever speak out as long as he lived. The sound of his own truthful statements confirmed his deliberate opinion that speech was of no use to him any longer" (p. 33). Additionally, one is reminded of Brierly's refusal to offer an explanatory suicide note, which helps prepare us for Jim's silence but carries also a stigma of overweening self-regard.

4. *Nostromo*: Versions of Failure

1. *Nostromo*, p. 84.
2. Jocelyn Baines, *Joseph Conrad: A Critical Biography* (New York: McGraw-Hill, 1960), p. 308.
3. Irving Howe, *Politics and the Novel* (New York: Horizon Press and Meridian Books, 1957), p. 109.
4. Ibid., p. 110.
5. Albert J. Guerard, *Conrad the Novelist* (Cambridge, Mass.: Harvard University Press, 1958), p. 199.
6. Howe, *Politics*, p. 112.
7. Guerard, *Conrad the Novelist*, p. 202.
8. Introduction, *Nostromo* (New York: The Modern Library, 1951), p. xxiii.
9. In this context, Conrad's familiar artistic claim to Sir Sidney Colvin, despite the voice of Conrad's public persona and the note of insistence, acquires a new depth and urgency: ". . . all my concern has been with the 'ideal' value of things, events, and people. That and nothing else. . . . *en vérité c'est les valeurs idéales des faits gestes humains qui se sont imposés à mon activité artistique.* Whatever narrative and dramatic gifts I may have are always, instinctively, used with that object—to get at, to bring forth *les valeurs idéales.*" Letter of March 18, 1917 in Georges Jean Aubry, *Joseph Conrad: Life and Letters*, vol. II (Garden City, N.Y.: Doubleday, 1927), p. 185.
10. Eloise Knapp Hay, *The Political Novels of Joseph Conrad* (Chicago: University of Chicago Press, 1963), p. 209.
11. Consider, for example, that the expansiveness and richness of *Nostromo* is soon followed by the bitterly satiric and enclosed world of *The Secret Agent*. A similar comparison holds for Melville's *Moby Dick* and *Pierre*, though *The Confidence Man* is closer in temper to *The Secret Agent*.
12. See Karen Horney, "The Idealized Image," in her *Our Inner Conflicts* (New York: Norton, 1945), pp. 96–114.
13. Guerard considers most of the third part of *Nostromo* inferior, a more sizable portion than I do. See Guerard, pp. 204–10. His detailed argument locates the fundamental defect in technique—point of view and distancing, whereas I see the problem as thematic, limited to Nostromo's downfall. Guerard appreciates a further difficulty: "The over-all weakness of the third section is puzzling and all the more because certain pages are brilliantly successful" (p. 206).

5. "The Secret Sharer": Affirmation of Action

1. Frederick R. Karl, *Joseph Conrad: The Three Lives* (New York: Farrar, Straus and Giroux, 1979), p. 675; Zdzislaw Najder, *Joseph Conrad: A Chronicle* (New Brunswick, N.J.: Rutgers University Press, 1983), p. 353.

2. Karl, *The Three Lives*, p. 677; Najder, *A Chronicle*, pp. 353–56.

3. Based on the dates of composition, Daleski observes that there is good reason to suppose that "Conrad urgently needed to write the story as a preliminary to undertaking the conclusion of the novel." H. M. Daleski, *Joseph Conrad: The Way of Dispossession* (New York: Holmes & Meier, 1977), p. 171. In explaining Conrad's imaginative necessity, however, I differ completely from Daleski.

4. "The Secret Sharer" in *'Twixt Land and Sea*, pp. 103–4.

5. "Leggatt is the captain's double and symbol for his unconscious, *but also a man of flesh and blood.*" Albert J. Guerard, Introduction, *"Heart of Darkness" and "The Secret Sharer"* (New York: The New American Library, Signet Edition, 1950), p. 12. Guerard's general statement on Leggatt seems to me to be the starting point for formulating a comprehensive reading of the story that does justice to its difficulty and its continuing interpretative problems.

6. Albert J. Guerard, *Conrad the Novelist* (Cambridge, Mass.: Harvard University Press, 1958), p. 22.

7. Guerard, Introduction, p. 11.

8. See Daniel Curley, "Legate of the Ideal," in *Conrad's "Secret Sharer" and the Critics*, ed. Bruce Harkness (Belmont, Calif.: Wadsworth Publishing, 1962); rpt. in *Conrad: A Collection of Critical Essays*, ed. Marvin Mudrick (Englewood Cliffs, N.J.: Prentice-Hall, 1966), pp. 75–82.

9. What is of consequence in this autobiographical rendering, according to Bernard Meyer, is not its veracity or romanticization, "for either hypothesis carries the same implication of Conrad's pronounced susceptibility, as a child and as a man, to the magnetic influence exerted by images epitomizing strength and masculinity." *Joseph Conrad. A Psychoanalytic Biography* (Princeton: Princeton University Press, 1967), p. 30. Najder concludes, though, that this episode of the Englishman on the Furca Pass is more Conrad's literary invention than a record of actual experience. "Conrad shapes the scene in his characteristic manner, trying to suggest after the fact that his life was subordinated to preconceived designs" (*A Chronicle*, pp. 36–37). Clearly, however, Conrad's treatment of this material does provide insight into his imagination and aids in interpreting his fiction.

10. Daniel Curley calls attention to Leggatt as the captain's perfect self-image, disputing Guerard's notion of him as a "criminally impulsive" self. "The basic error," Curley goes on to say, "is not in equating Leggatt with the captain's instinctive self but in equating *instinctive* with *evil*" ("Legate of the Ideal," p. 81). However, Curley understates Leggatt's crime and the violence inherent in his instinctual vigor.

11. Donald Yelton, *Mimesis and Metaphor* (The Hague: Mouton, 1967), p. 281.

12. Daleski, p. 173.

13. "The Shadow Line" elaborates the insidious physical and spiritual effects of this gulf calm.

14. It is worth observing that Marlow does not—cannot—judge Kurtz.

15. This view is advanced, for example, by Carl Benson, "Conrad's Two Stories of Initiation," *PMLA* 69 (March 1954): 45–56, and by Yelton, p. 289. Benson contends that the captain has demonstrated his authority in a "needlessly fear-inspiring way" (p. 48). He contradicts the work's seemingly positive conclusion, viewing the protagonist's assurance as ill-founded, his initiation into maturity as "humanly abortive" because he has not yet reached the stage of human solidarity. Rather, Benson continues, the adult moral corrective to this commander's incomplete growth is presented in his counterpart's drama in "The Shadow Line," where the captain's experience provides

a keen understanding of the inadequacy of self-sufficiency. However, the telling moral comparison is better made with Archbold than with a character outside the story, and Benson underplays the esthetic consideration that the later fiction is a conservative, diluted reworking of material in "The Secret Sharer," inferior as imaginative literature.

16. J. L. Simmons maintains that the tale's affirmation has to do with the ideal nature of Leggatt and with the commitment of both doubles to the morality of the sea—simple, straightforward, elemental—as opposed to the morality of the land— complex, action-inhibiting, debatable—personified in Archbold. See his "The Dual Morality in 'The Secret Sharer,'" *Studies in Short Fiction* 2 (Spring 1965): 209–20. But Simmons sides too easily with the young officers so that his reading lacks an essential skepticism. Conrad's endorsement of a "sea morality" is by no means simple. Moral complexity is evident, for example, in the fact that Leggatt's criminal violence derives from the instinctive strength that led to his heroism, in Conrad's terms of punishment for his outcast. Moreover, those dutiful mariners who receive Conrad's highest praise also possess, unlike the captain and Leggatt, consciousness and an appreciation of the darker facets of life, e.g., the French lieutenant of *Lord Jim*.

17. Porter Williams, Jr., "The Matter of Conscience in Conrad's *The Secret Sharer*," *PMLA* 79 (December 1964): 629.

18. Guerard, *Conrad the Novelist*, pp. 23–24.

19. Daleski, p. 183. Williams regards the hat's appearance as Leggatt's deliberate act, a redemptive gesture that contributes to the work's optimistic finale. "Just as the original Cain set out to take his punishment and meet a new destiny with the confidence that something has been done for him to make that punishment endurable [Cain had asked for protection and received it from God, Leggatt from the Captain], so our new Cain sets out in the same way but with the additional confidence that he had himself done something for his own redemption," that is, left behind the hat as a marker to aid the commander in his danger (Porter Williams, Jr., "The Brand of Cain in 'The Secret Sharer,'" *Modern Fiction Studies* 10 [Spring 1964]: 30). Failing to consider how the swimmer is not "free," Williams accept a literal reading of the story's last sentence. That Leggatt leaves the hat in the water because he knows the captain's predicament strains credibility.

20. Expansionist and romantic impulses are freed and "legitimized" for Marlow, Jim, and Nostromo when, for one reason or another, these seamen are separated from a rigorous service. They become respectively Congo steamboat captain, Lord in Patusan, indispensable Capataz after jumping ship in Costaguana.

6. *Under Western Eyes*: Integrity Achieved

1. Author's Note to *Under Western Eyes*, p. viii.

2. Conrad is ironic, for this praise of philosophic independence can be read pejoratively, as a fastidious, proud detachment from human involvement.

3. Albert J. Guerard, *Conrad the Novelist* (Cambridge, Mass.: Harvard University Press, 1958), p. 243.

4. Zdzislaw Najder, *Joseph Conrad: A Chronicle* (New Brunswick, N.J.: Rutgers University Press, 1983), p. 44ff.

5. Edward Crankshaw, "Conrad and Russia," in *Joseph Conrad: A Commemoration, Papers from the 1974 International Conference on Conrad,* Canterbury, England, 1974, ed. Norman Sherry (New York: Barnes & Noble Books, Harper & Row, 1977), p. 93.

6. Solzhenitsyn's first-hand account of the recruitment of camp informers, including a near-successful attempt to enlist him, reveals how fully Conrad has imagined Mikulin's seduction of Razumov. See Aleksandr I. Solzhenitsyn, *The Gulag Archipelago 1918–1956: An Experiment in Literary Investigation,* vols. III–IV, trans. Thomas P. Whitney (New York: Harper & Row, 1975), pp. 353–74.

7. Guerard, *Conrad the Novelist,* p. 235.

8. Ibid., p. 236.

9. Yuri Zhivago in Pasternak's novel speaks eloquently to an ailing patient about the soul. "However far back you go in your memory, it is always in some external, active manifestation of yourself that you come across your identity—in the work of your hands, in your family, in other people. . . . You in others—this is your soul. This is what you are. This is what your consciousness has breathed and lived on and enjoyed throughout your life—your soul, your immortality, your life in others. And what now? You have always been in others and you will remain in others. And what does it matter to you if later on that is called your memory? This will be you—the you that enters the future and becomes a part of it." Boris Pasternak, *Doctor Zhivago,* trans. Max Hayward and Manya Harari (New York: The Modern Library, 1958), p. 68.

10. See Jocelyn Baines, *Joseph Conrad: A Critical Biography* (New York: McGraw-Hill, 1960), pp. 53–54; Adam Gillon, *The Eternal Solitary: A Study of Joseph Conrad* (New York: Bookman Associates, 1960), pp. 112–16; Bernard Meyer, *Joseph Conrad: A Psychoanalytic Biography* (Princeton: Princeton University Press, 1967), pp. 36–39; Frederick R. Karl, *Joseph Conrad: The Three Lives* (New York: Farrar, Straus and Giroux, 1979), pp. 125–27; Najder, *A Chronicle,* pp. 47–53.

11. Irving Howe, *Politics and the Novel* (New York: Horizon Press and Meridian Books, 1957), p. 92.

12. Frederick R. Karl, *A Reader's Guide to Joseph Conrad,* rev. ed. (New York: Farrar, Straus and Giroux, 1969), p. 224.

13. See Ludwik Krzyżanowski, "Joseph Conrad's 'Prince Roman': Fact and Fiction," in *Joseph Conrad: Centennial Essays,* ed. Ludwik Krzyżanowski (New York: The Polish Institute of Arts and Sciences in America, 1960), pp. 27–72. Prince Sanguszko soldiered with Conrad's grandfather Korzeniowski, and Conrad was originally to have included material on the prince in his memoirs (Karl, *The Three Lives,* pp. 69, 688). This fact and the air of recollection in the tale hint strongly that the boy meeting the deaf prince is actually Conrad, who in 1867 did in fact meet the prince.

14. Krzyżanowski, p. 58.

15. In reality, the prince's term of exile was fifteen years, though he remained deprived of his title and civil rights until 1856 (Krzyżanowski, p. 59). Conrad's extension of the time seems to be an oversight. I might add that Conrad would not revisit Poland until 1914, three years after writing this story, ending an absence of twenty-one years.

Index